Contents

Chapter 1: Pros & Cons of Plant-based Diets

Chapter 2: Dietary Trends

Introduction

Plant-based Diets is Volume 421 in the issues series. The aim of the series is to offer current, diverse information about important issues in our world, from a UK perspective.

About Plant-based Diets

17% of Brits have reduced their consumption of animal products over the past decade. Widely accepted as a healthier choice and better for the planet, the growing trend for ethical, alternative diets is perhaps unsurprising. This book looks at the pros and cons of alternative diets and the reasons behind the rising inclination to eat more plants and less meat.

Our sources

Titles in the issues series are designed to function as educational resource books, providing a balanced overview of a specific subject.

The information in our books is comprised of facts, articles and opinions from many different sources, including:

- Newspaper reports and opinion pieces
- Website factsheets
- Magazine and journal articles
- Statistics and surveys
- Government reports
- Literature from special interest groups.

A note on critical evaluation

Because the information reprinted here is from a number of different sources, readers should bear in mind the origin of the text and whether the source is likely to have a particular bias when presenting information (or when conducting their research). It is hoped that, as you read about the many aspects of the issues explored in this book, you will critically evaluate the information presented.

It is important that you decide whether you are being presented with facts or opinions. Does the writer give a biased or unbiased report? If an opinion is being expressed, do you agree with the writer? Is there potential bias to the 'facts' or statistics behind an article?

Activities

Throughout this book, you will find a selection of assignments and activities designed to help you engage with the articles you have been reading and to explore your own opinions. Some tasks will take longer than others and there is a mixture of design, writing and research-based activities that you can complete alone or in a group.

Further research

At the end of each article we have listed its source and a website that you can visit if you would like to conduct your own research. Please remember to critically evaluate any sources that you consult and consider whether the information you are viewing is accurate and unbiased.

Issues Online

The **issues** series of books is complimented by our online resource, issuesonline.co.uk

On the Issues Online website you will find a wealth of information, covering over 70 topics, to support the PSHE and RSE curriculum.

Why Issues Online?

Researching a topic? Issues Online is the best place to start for...

Librarians

Issues Online is an essential tool for librarians: feel confident you are signposting safe, reliable, user-friendly online resources to students and teaching staff alike. We provide multi-user concurrent access, so no waiting around for another student to finish with a resource. Issues Online also provides FREE downloadable posters for your shelf/wall/table displays.

Teachers

Issues Online is an ideal resource for lesson planning, inspiring lively debate in class and setting lessons and homework tasks.

Our accessible, engaging content helps deepen student's knowledge, promotes critical thinking and develops independent learning skills.

Issues Online saves precious preparation time. We wade through the wealth of material on the internet to filter the best quality, most relevant and up-to-date information you need to start exploring a topic.

Our carefully selected, balanced content presents an overview and insight into each topic from a variety of sources and viewpoints.

Students

Issues Online is designed to support your studies in a broad range of topics, particularly social issues relevant to young people today.

Thousands of articles, statistics and infographs instantly available to help you with research and assignments.

With 24/7 access using the powerful Algolia search system, you can find relevant information quickly, easily and safely anytime from your laptop, tablet or smartphone, in class or at home.

Visit issuesonline.co.uk to find out more!

What are the health benefits of a plant-based diet?

By Emily Brennan

Lots of people want to include more fruit and vegetables into their diets for all sorts of reasons, but the health benefits of eating a balanced, plant-based diet are increasingly difficult to ignore.

By shifting the focus of your diet away from meat, dairy and eggs, and towards fruits, vegetables, wholegrains, beans, pulses, seeds and nuts in their natural and unprocessed forms, you'll unlock a whole host of health benefits.

Not only will you naturally start to become more aware of what an amazing variety of produce is available, along with all the delicious recipes and flavour combinations you can explore, but you'll also discover the positive effects it can have on your health in both short and long term.

For clarity, in this article we are talking about whole plant-based foods in their natural and unprocessed forms, for example a sweet potato prepared and cooked at home, rather than a packet of sweet potato fries from the supermarket.

So, what are some of the health benefits of joining the plant-based revolution?

Better digestion

Eating a plant-based diet that includes a variety of wholegrains, legumes, vegetables, and fruit is a huge advantage for your digestive system, as it increases the diversity of your gut microbiome, according to a study published in 2017. This can lead to improved gut health, and, as a result, better overall health and wellness.

The fibre factor

Plant-based foods are also naturally high in fibre, and according to the British Nutrition Foundation, most adults are only getting about two-thirds of the daily recommended fibre intake in their diets. Fibre is found naturally in plant-based foods, and by consuming these in their natural form it can lead to a number of health benefits, including lower cholesterol, better bowel health, and more stable blood sugar levels.

More energy

By replacing sugary, processed snacks with plant-based alternatives, you'll start to notice improved focus and better concentration to see you through the day. For example, if you replace that mid-morning chocolate biscuit with a handful of mixed nuts, you'll notice that the energy will be released slowly and steadily rather than in a quick release of sugar followed by a crash. One of my favourite afternoon snacks is a sliced apple with nut butter, which stops any crisp cravings in their tracks and leaves me feeling full until dinner.

Improved heart health

According to the World Health Organization, in 2020 heart disease was the number one cause of death worldwide, responsible for 16% of the world's total deaths. It's usually associated with a build-up of fatty deposits within the arteries and an increased risk of blood clots. However, a 2019 study from the Journal of the American Heart Association found that middle-aged adults who ate diets higher in plant-based foods and lower in animal products had a lower risk of heart disease.

Diabetes management and prevention

In 2009, a study of 60,000 people showed only 2.9% of people on a vegan diet had type 2 diabetes, compared to 7.6% of those eating a non-vegetarian diet. A 2018 review suggests that adopting a plant-based diet could help people with diabetes achieve and maintain a healthy weight, and better manage their medication requirements.

Reduced risk of some cancers

Leaving processed red meats like bacon, sausages, hot dogs, and cured meats off your plate, means you'll be cutting out a whole range of foods that have been categorised as Group 1 carcinogens by the International Agency for Research on Cancer (IARC).

Better skin

Fruits and vegetables have a high water-content, and consuming more of them, more often, means your skin will look brighter and more hydrated. There is also growing evidence to support a whole-food plant-based diet in the prevention of skin ageing.

Better sleep

Maybe it's knowing that their food choices have had a positive impact on their overall health, but many followers of plant-based diets report improved sleep patterns. The good news is that tryptophan, which plays a role in both the production of serotonin, a mood stabiliser, and melatonin, which helps regulate sleep patterns, can be found in several plant-based foods including nuts and leafy greens.

Want to eat more plant-based?

There are plenty of great health reasons to try including more plant-based meals in your diet. Not only that, but eating less meat means fewer animals in factory farms, lower water consumption, and a lower impact on climate change.

If you're still unsure, why not spend a weekend trying out some new plant-based recipes that contain only natural, unprocessed ingredients? Or how about dedicating just one day a week to eating only plant-based meals?

Plant-based options are growing

You don't have to eat only whole plant-based foods to still do good for yourself and the world. There are so many other great plant-based products out there, ranging from meat-free burgers to dairy-free chocolates and cheeses. When enjoyed as part of a balanced diet, these foods are super tasty and better for animals and the environment.

7 April 2022

Key Facts

- According to the British Nutrition Foundation, most adults are only getting about two-thirds of the daily recommended fibre intake in their diets.

- According to the World Health Organization, in 2020 heart disease was the number one cause of death worldwide, responsible for 16% of the world's total deaths.

Brainstorming

Why is a healthy diet important?

List 4 health benefits of a plant-based diet

www.thehumaneleague.org.uk

Meet Britain's vegans & vegetarians

YouGov talks to 1,000 Britons who have given up eating meat.

By Sarah Prescott-Smith, Senior Research Executive and Matthew Smith, Head of Data Journalism

The first month of the year sees many people embark on a 'Veganuary' adventure, trying to follow a plant-based diet for the duration of January. Those seeking to eat without meat are becoming increasingly well catered for, with food delivery service Deliveroo showing that around 15,000 restaurants across the UK added plant-based dishes to their standard menus in 2021.

Now a new YouGov survey of 1,000 vegans and vegetarians provides unique insights to these groups, asking, among other things, what motivated them to start, how they practise their beliefs, and what their experience has been like.

How many vegans and vegetarians are there in Britain?

Britain's vegan and vegetarian population remains small. YouGov tracker data over the last two and a half years puts the size of the vegan population at about 2-3% and the vegetarian population at about 5-7%.

Our dedicated survey of vegans and vegetarians shows that most of Britain's vegans are pretty new to the lifestyle, with 63% having started out only in the last five years. That being said, the overwhelming majority of Britain's vegans (81%) graduated from vegetarianism, so many have been avoiding meat for much longer than this.

There are plenty of newbie vegetarians as well, with 46% having cut all meat out of their diet in the last five years.

Why do people become vegan or vegetarian?

Unsurprisingly, the top reasons people originally became vegetarian or vegan are not wanting to eat animals or animal products (63% of vegetarians and 70% of vegans) and believing that the way animals are raised and killed for food is cruel (59% and 80% respectively).

These motivations are even higher when asked their reasons for remaining vegan or vegetarian, suggesting that some people get into the diet or lifestyle for some reasons and

Why do people become vegan/vegetarian?

Why did you orginally become a vegan/vegetarian? and for what reasons are you currently a vegan/vegetarian?
Please select all that apply. % of 274 vegans and 733 vegetarians.

Vegans | **Vegetarians**

I don't want to eat animals or animal products — Vegans: 70 / 88; Vegetarians: 63 / 77

I think the way animals are farmed and killed for food is cruel — Vegans: 80 / 89; Vegetarians: 59 / 70

Environmental reasons — Vegans: 53 / 79; Vegetarians: 32 / 52

Personal health reasons — Vegans: 27 / 40; Vegetarians: 13 / 20

I was raised vegan/vegetarian by my parents/guardians — Vegans: 5 / 6; Vegetarians: 11 / 9

Because someone else wanted me to (e.g. my partner) — Vegans: 5 / 4; Vegetarians: 3 / 2

Religious reasons — Vegans: 1 / 2; Vegetarians: 4 / 3

Other — Vegans: 9 / 7; Vegetarians: 12 / 12

Current reasons (green) · Original reasons (purple)

Source: YouGov - 13-27 December 2021

then, as they learn more, incorporate extra motivations into their personal philosophy as well.

With many environmental organisations calling for a shift to more plant-based eating, half of vegans (53%) and a third of vegetarians (32%) say their concerns for Mother Earth were a prompt for originally going vegan. The environmental factor sees the largest increase between how many set out originally because of environmental concerns and how many say it's become a motivation for continuing to do so (79% of vegans and 52% of vegetarians).

Health was also cited as a key reason by a quarter of vegans (27%) and one in eight vegetarians (13%) starting out on a meat-free diet for this reason. The same survey shows that seven in ten vegans and a third of vegetarians say their health has improved as a result of their diet, which could be part of the reason the number of people saying health is a current reason they practise veganism or vegetarianism has increased to 40% and 20% respectively.

What else do people practise as part of their vegetarian or vegan lifestyle?

While the dietary aspects are the most obvious part of the vegetarian and vegan lifestyle, for many it extends beyond just what they put on their plate.

Some nine in ten vegans (92%) say they avoid beauty and hygiene products that may have been tested on animals, as do 79% of vegetarians.

When it comes to clothing, 70% of vegetarians and 74% of vegans avoid purchasing new products with real animal fur, with similar numbers (67% and 71%) refusing to buy second hand fur products also.

There is a much more noticeable split between groups when it comes to leather. While 68% of vegans won't buy new leather items, putting it on a par with animal fur, this figure falls to just 51% of vegetarians. Likewise, when it comes to second hand leather, vegans (57%) are substantially more likely to boycott it than vegetarians (39%).

Vegans are also far more likely to evangelize about the benefits of the lifestyle than vegetarians: 61% of vegans say they encourage friends and family to make lifestyle changes, compared to 37% of vegetarians.

Is it ok for vegans and vegetarians to eat lab-grown meat?

Recent years have seen a surge of investment in attempts to get lab-grown meat out to market, with supporters arguing that it will produce meat without the need to farm and slaughter an animal and with far less of an environmental impact.

Vegetarians and vegans aren't certain on whether it would be acceptable for them to eat lab grown meat, with 42% of vegetarians and 35% of vegans saying it would be unacceptable. Still, 34% of vegetarians and 30% of vegans think it would be ok for someone with their respective diets to eat meat grown from embryos. Around 24-29% are still unsure on the morality of the question, however.

Is it OK for vegans and vegetarians to eat insects?

For many people who are concerned about the sustainability of their food, insects have been cited as a more environmentally friendly way to get protein and other essential vitamins than eating meat. However, 82% of vegans and 83% of vegetarians think it'd be unacceptable for them to eat insects. Only 9% of vegetarians, and 5% of vegans, think it would be ok to incorporate them into their diets.

Is it ok for vegans and vegetarians to eat wild animals that died of natural causes?

Because so many vegans and vegetarians stopped eating meat because of the kind of conditions farmed animals are put through, is it philosophically acceptable to eat animals that weren't raised or killed specifically to be food?

Seemingly not, with the vast majority of vegans and vegetarians (77-82%) saying it would be unacceptable to eat wild animals that had died of natural causes.

Is it ok for vegans and vegetarians to wear leather?

Seven in ten vegans (70%) and a majority of vegetarians (56%) say wearing newly-made leather products is unacceptable.

Is it ok for vegans to eat honey or ride horses?

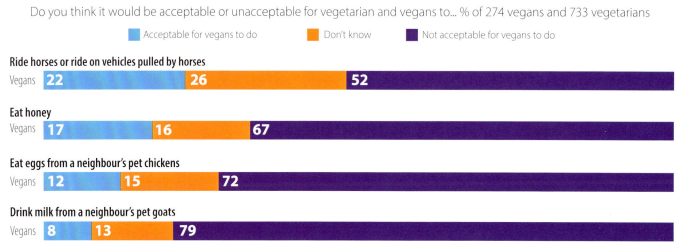

Do you think it would be acceptable or unacceptable for vegetarian and vegans to... % of 274 vegans and 733 vegetarians

Acceptable for vegans to do · Don't know · Not acceptable for vegans to do

Ride horses or ride on vehicles pulled by horses
Vegans 22 | 26 | 52

Eat honey
Vegans 17 | 16 | 67

Eat eggs from a neighbour's pet chickens
Vegans 12 | 15 | 72

Drink milk from a neighbour's pet goats
Vegans 8 | 13 | 79

Source: YouGov 13-27 December 2021

Half of vegans and two in five vegetarians face hostility or disapproval from at least some of their friends and family over their lifestyle choice

Thinking about the following groups of people in your life, how many, if any, express disapproval or hostility towards your choice to be vegan/vegetarian? % of 274 vegans and 733 vegetarians.

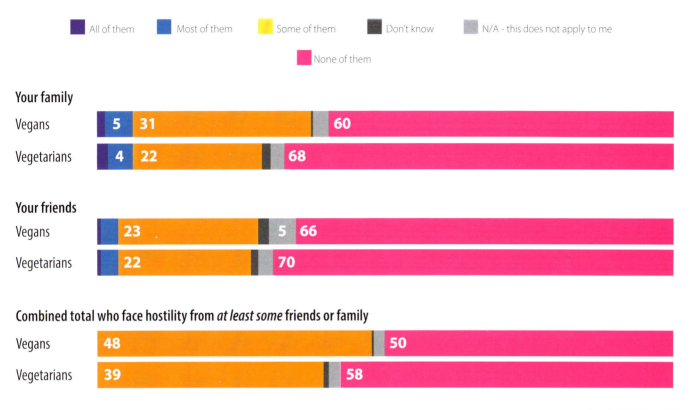

Source: YouGov 13-27 December 2021

Nevertheless, a third of vegetarians think such garments are acceptable for vegetarians (33%). A mere 1% of vegans say they should be able to wear new leather (although 21% see nothing wrong with vegetarians being able to do so.

Attitudes are more lenient when it comes to second hand leather clothing, which 50% of vegetarians and 31% of vegans say would be ok for their own groups to wear. Only a third from each group (33-34%) think it is unacceptable to wear second hand leather.

Is it ok for vegans to eat honey?

A key tenet of vegan belief that separates it from vegetarianism is that not only should people not eat animals but they should also not benefit from animal labour.

Perhaps the most well-known example of this is that vegans aren't supposed to eat honey, something which two thirds of vegans we asked (67%) say is unacceptable. Half (52%) also say it is wrong for vegans to ride horses or to use vehicles pulled by horses, compared to 22% who think this is ok.

Are imitation meat and dairy products as good as the real thing?

Recent years have seen a proliferation of new meat-free and dairy-free imitation products, aimed not just at vegans and vegetarians but also at those with specific intolerances.

While companies are working hard at making these products as realistic as possible, there is still some way to go. Of the types of imitation food we asked about, vegan substitute chicken comes closes to matching the real thing, although just 10% of vegans and vegetarians proclaim it 'basically identical'. A majority (55%) do say it is at least 'fairly close', however.

Dairy products seem to have been harder to nail down, particularly cheese. Fully 45% describe the current market of fake cheeses to be 'not very close' or 'not close at all' to the real deal, outnumbering the 35% who see them as at least fairly close.

Replacements for cow's milk also score relatively poorly, with 32% saying they aren't much like the real thing.

How many vegans and vegetarians face hostility from friends and family?

The results show that half of vegans (48%) and four in ten vegetarians (39%) face disapproval or hostility from at least some of their family or friends about their lifestyle choice.

Vegans are more likely to say they face negativity from family members (37%) than friends (27%), while among vegetarians these figures are about the same (29% and 26%).

20 January 2022

Climate-friendly diets can make a huge difference – even if you don't go all-out vegan

Changing habits can be hard but even partial shifts from meat-based menus could significantly decrease planet-heating emissions.

By Amanda Schupak

Who chooses what you eat? If your answer is 'I do,' you're partly right. You may buy your own groceries and order your own restaurant meals, but it's the food industry that determines what is stocked on store shelves and listed on menus.

'The institutions all around us affect food choice,' said Matthew Hayek, assistant professor of environmental studies at New York University. Your choices are whittled down by what's in the supermarket, your workplace or school canteen, the restaurants in the strip mall on your way home, he said.

That means that for people who want to reduce the carbon footprint of their diets, the greenest option isn't always on the table. Or if it is, it isn't the most appetizing or convenient.

What we eat has an enormous environmental impact. Scientists estimate that food production causes 35% of planet-warming greenhouse gas emissions, with meat responsible for more than twice the pollution of fruits, grains and greens.

In April, the Intergovernmental Panel on Climate Change (IPCC) report urged world leaders, especially those in developed countries, to support a transition to sustainable, healthy, low-emissions diets to help mitigate the worst effects of the climate crisis.

But the burden can't rest on individuals making personal food choices, experts stress – producers, retailers,

restaurants, workplaces and government must help make plant-based foods convenient, enticing and tasty.

'It's hard for people to change their diets'

Eating less meat is one of the most meaningful changes people can make to curb greenhouse gas emissions, help reduce deforestation and even decrease the risk of pandemic-causing diseases passing from animals to humans, according to the IPCC report.

The shifts needn't be extreme. Adopting a healthy Mediterranean-style diet – rich in grains, vegetables, nuts and moderate amounts of fish and poultry – could be nearly as effective as going vegetarian or vegan, the report found. If everyone met basic nutritional recommendations, which for most people in developed countries means more fruit and veg and less red meat, emissions could fall 29% by 2050, according to one study.

'But it's hard for people to change their diets,' said Caroline Bushnell at the Good Food Institute, a non-profit that advocates for plant-based and cultured meat.

Consumers often say they're motivated to eat more healthily and more sustainably. But if given the choice between a dish that's better for the planet but not especially appetizing, and a mouth-watering, meat-heavy option, people tend to listen to their gut, not their conscience.

Food emissions in the highest emitting economies in 2019, per capita

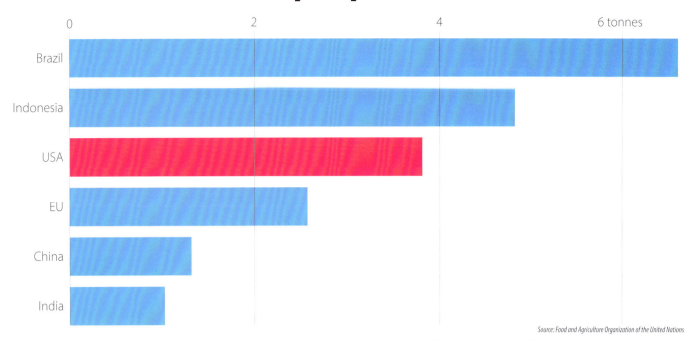

Source: Food and Agriculture Organization of the United Nations

Emissions from producing animal-based food

Beef accounts for over 4.2bn metric tonnes of global carbon emissions

Source: Xu, X., et al. Nature Food (2021)

It's like offering someone the choice between fries and a side salad, Bushnell said. 'Most people don't pick the side salad – it's not really an equivalent option.'

GFI wants large food manufacturers and processors to 'change how the foods that people love are made', she said. 'Instead of advocating for behaviour change, we approach it from a supply side angle.'

Big meat companies and consumer food brands are banking on plant-based proteins and lab-grown meat to help them respond to a growing appetite for more climate-friendly foods and to cut their own emissions.

McDonald's is testing out the McPlant, while Burger King sells Impossible Whoppers and its UK arm is aiming for half of its menu to be plant-based by 2030. Ikea has promised the same in its restaurants by 2025.

Perdue makes hybrid chicken-veggie nuggets for kids and Tyson, which now calls itself a 'protein' company, has launched its own brand of plant-based products. Last year JBS, the world's largest meat producer, acquired a cultivated meat startup and plans to start selling lab-grown steaks, sausages and hamburgers in 2024.

Supermarket tactics

With more products to sell, retailers, too, need to push non-animal proteins. The UK's largest supermarket chain, Tesco, for example, set a five-year goal to increase sales of plant-based proteins by 300%.

Getting customers to put plant-based alternatives in their shopping carts starts with placing those products next to things they're alternative to, Bushnell said – meat-free burgers near the ground beef, vegan cheeses among conventional goudas and mozzarella – rather than relegating them to a speciality section.

Placement in the refrigerated section was crucial to bringing alternative milks mainstream. The tactic was pioneered in the 1990s by the founder of Silk, who started packaging his company's soy milk in traditional milk cartons and persuading grocery stores to stock them in the dairy case. Now cow milks mingle with a bevy of nut and grain milks and 90% of alternative milk sales come from the fridge rather than the shelf-stable aisle.

The infiltration of alternative protein companies into supermarket real estate has not been without pushback, however. Several states, with pressure from farm associations, have passed laws restricting the use of words such as 'burger', 'sausage' and 'hotdog' on plant-based products, on the basis they could mislead customers. A similar law was voted down in the EU, though the bloc still prohibits labeling vegan products with dairy names.

'Consumers are not confused,' Bushnell said. 'They don't think when they buy a plant-based hotdog it's a beef hotdog, but they understand how to use it.'

Food choices are rarely rational

In 2020, the research non-profit the World Resources Institute released a report looking at the most effective ways to encourage people to eat less meat based on the psychology of food choices. One of the strongest conclusions, the researchers wrote, was 'that decision-making around what to eat is rarely a rational and carefully thought-through process'. People crave familiarity and are influenced by subtle physical and linguistic cues.

The report advises those in the food industry to offer more plant-based options, make them taste good and make them sound good. While fried chicken is 'crispy' and burgers are 'juicy', menus often describe plant-based options as 'healthy', 'vegan' or 'meat-free' – none of which, research shows, makes people want to order them.

Using language to evoke flavour and mouthfeel (rather than healthfulness or ethics) makes people substantially more likely to order a vegetarian meal. When the cafes of UK food retailer Sainsbury's renamed their meat-free sausage and

mashed potatoes 'Cumberland spiced veggie sausage and mash', sales shot up 76%.

Other linguistic nudges can promote veg options by highlighting their environmental benefits. Among the most effective messages in WRI's research were calls for people to be part of something already happening: '90% of Americans are making the change to eat less meat. Join this growing movement.' Or they were easy to understand comparisons: 'swapping just one meat dish for a plant-based one saves greenhouse gas emissions that are equivalent to the energy used to charge your phone for two years.'

'Both of those are all about making an inconsequential choice a bit more consequential,' said Sophie Attwood, a senior behavioral scientist at WRI.

It also helps, Attwood said, to put vegetable options at the top of the menu and interspersed with, rather than segregated from, meat dishes. Studies have found making vegetable meals the default choice makes people many times more likely to order them.

Companies and institutions can lower their emissions by offering more plant-based meals. 'They are the most important changes that an organization can make. What are you serving? What's the ratio of vegetarian to meat-based dishes?' said Edwina Hughes, head of WRI's cool food program, which has pledges from more than 50 organizations to reduce the climate impact of their food by 25% by 2030.

But some experts say real change needs to include legislative measures, such as taxing meat, as some European countries are considering. It seems unlikely in the US even though one study found more than a third of Americans would support it, even as inflation pushes up food prices.

Making progress requires all the tools available, said Hayek: educating people about food's climate impact; giving them more and better plant-based options; guiding choice by changing the default, offering incentives and imposing disincentives (such as taxes); restricting and in some cases eliminating most meat options (as some European universities have). It worked to curb smoking rates, Hayek said, and it could work for food.

'What does it look like if we actually dedicate ourselves to making a concerted, comprehensive attempt to tackle food choices?' he asked. 'Let's try.'

4 June 2022

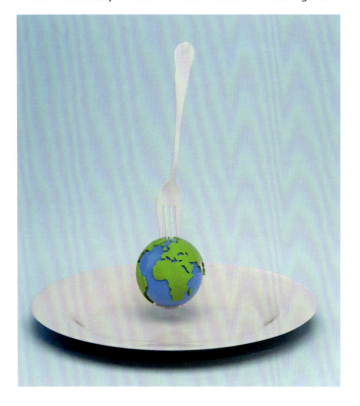

Vegetarian & vegan diet pros & cons

By Danny Webber

What is a vegan diet?

A vegan diet is a plant-based lifestyle that prohibits the consumption of all animal products, with many people adopting a vegan diet for health, environmental and strong ethical beliefs concerning animal welfare.

Strict vegans will also avoid using any products that have been tested on animals or wear leather or wool. So is a vegan diet healthy? What are the vegan diet pros and cons? Let's find out in this comprehensive guide!

Vegetarianism/ veganism pros and cons

Vegetarian & vegan diets are more popular than ever, particularly for athletes in an attempt to maximize performance.

There are many benefits of a plant-based diet, and they are claimed to be the healthiest diet to follow because they prioritise naturally sourced plant-based foods (fruits and vegetables, legumes, and whole grains).

This is great and exactly how all diets should be but are there any downsides to a plant-based diet? Just to be clear, I am in no way against a vegan diet plan. I just want to outline any potential risks and help all athletes who choose to adopt a plant-based diet to get the best results.

Other pros and cons of veganism

Apart from the discussed pros and cons of veganism on page 10, there are some other significant benefits and drawbacks of being vegan. Let's find them out:

Pros of being vegan

Helps to reduce the risk of cardiovascular and heart disease: One of the significant contributing elements to heart disease is your diet. The vegan diet prioritises a wealth of natural, nutrient-dense plant-based foods that promote heart health. Whole grains, fruits, vegetables, legumes, nuts, seeds, etc., all have excellent health properties.

The research of 126 omnivorous men and 170 vegetarians showed that those who adopted a vegetarian diet had lower blood pressure and a lower probability of coronary heart disease.

Helps to improve blood sugar levels: Type 2 diabetes is a global health issue. However, some studies show that a vegan diet plays a specific role in improving blood sugar levels. It typically reduces the intake of poor-quality processed foods overconsumed in typical Western diets that contributes to type 2 diabetes.

Reference: https://www.mdpi.com/2072-6643/6/11/4822/htm

Other disadvantages of vegan diet

Potential nutritional deficiency: A vegan diet may lack some of the critical nutrients required for the body, such as protein, vitamin B-12, omega-3 fatty acids, zinc, and iron.

Following a vegan diet requires knowing about the key foods that should be combined together and prioritised to sufficiently meet these nutrient intakes, and analysing your diet (with the help of a registered dietitian/nutritionist), to see if you require any additional supplements to prevent

Advantages & disadvantages of being vegan

Advantages	Disadvantages
Obtain a variety of fruits and vegetables each day	Vegan diets can be low in protein and fat
Useful diet for weight loss	Common nutrient deficiencies
Increased feelings of satiety (high food volume, low energy intake)	
High intake of fibre	Vegans have more trouble achieving protein needs without using protein supplements
Will have no issues meeting daily protein requirements (this is one of the benefits of a vegetarian but not vegan diet)	When dieting, especially in athletes, higher protein intakes are advised to promote muscle retention and recovery, combat hunger, and enhance mood
Naturally high carbohydrate diets to support endurance training	Vegans, therefore, need more protein as the protein quality of diet is lower compared to vegetarian and meat-eaters

Source: Webber Nutrition

any nutrient deficiencies if you struggle to obtain these nutrients through food alone.

Reference: https://sciendo.com/pdf/10.2478/arls-2019-0010

On the fence: neither pros or cons of vegetarianism:

This means that the vegan diet pros and cons balance each other out. Well-designed vegetarian and vegan diet recipes neither hinder nor aid performance compared to an already well-structured diet that includes animal products.

Common nutrient deficiencies on a vegan diet/ vegetarian diet

Vegetarian and Vegan diets are undoubtedly beneficial for your health, but completely cutting off animal products from your diet might result in some common nutritional deficiencies.

The most common nutritional deficiencies in vegan and vegetarian diets include:

- Vit B12 (both should supplement)
- Vit D3 (EVERYONE should supplement)
- Calcium (plant sources may limit absorption, the only issue for non-dairy consumers)
- Iron (high in iron, but absorption may be the issue, include Vitamin C foods with meals and/or supplements (all non-red meat eaters; female vegan endurance athletes at high risk of anemia)

- Zinc (a potential problem for vegans)
- Iodine (potential issue for non-seafood/dairy/egg eaters)
- Omega-3 (non-fish eaters will need to supplement – algae-based EPA/DHA)

Let us now find out vegan sources for the above-mentioned deficiencies:

Vegan sources of calcium

- Dark leafy green vegetables, e.g. broccoli, kale, and cabbage. Tofu.
- Calcium-fortified cereals, milk, and bread.
- Dried fruits.
- Sesame seeds/hummus.

Vegan sources of Vitamin D

- Direct sunlight to skin.
- Fortified fat spreads, breakfast cereals, and unsweetened soya drinks.
- Vitamin D3 supplements.

Vegan sources of Iron

- Pulses.
- Wholemeal bread and flour.
- Breakfast cereals are fortified with Iron. Dark green, leafy vegetables, such as watercress, broccoli, and spring greens.

- Nuts.
- Dried fruits, such as apricots, prunes, and figs.

Vegan sources of Vitamin B12

- Breakfast cereals fortified with B12.
- Unsweetened soy drinks fortified with vitamin B12.
- Yeast extract, such as Marmite, is fortified with vitamin B12.

Vegan sources of Omega-3 Fatty Acids

- Walnuts & flaxseeds.
- Tofu.
- Vegan Omega 3 supplement.

What are the different types of vegetarian diets?

The main types of plant-based diets are:

- Vegan – no animal products
- Vegetarian/Lacto-Ovo vegetarian – includes dairy and eggs
  - Ovo vegetarian – no dairy
  - Lacto vegetarian – no eggs
- Pescatarian – includes fish, dairy and eggs
- Flexitarian – includes small amounts of all animal products.

What's the difference between a vegan diet and a plant-based diet?

Vegan diets will eliminate all animal products and by-products, whereas plant-based or vegetarian diets may often include dairy sources, eggs, and small portions of white meat and fish.

Is veganism right for me?

Veganism is only right for you if you adopt it for the right reasons to support environmental and ethical beliefs and find it sustainable as part of your lifestyle and food preferences.

Take-home messages:

1. Protein intake needs to be considered – combine different plant-based protein foods to complement their amino acid profiles for more complete proteins.
2. May limit food options on social occasions.
3. Vegan/plant-based diets can significantly increase the nutritional quality of a person's diet, mainly those who have swapped from a highly processed, westernised diet with little amounts of fruit and veg.
4. Many health benefits to a plant-based diet for weight loss, health and athletic performance and recovery.
5. Be wary of nutrient deficiencies & supplements where needed.
6. Female athletes (especially vegans) should be checked for iron-deficiency anaemia.

10 August 2022

FAQs:

Can you get enough protein on a vegetarian diet?

Yes, you can get enough protein in a vegetarian diet. Dairy and eggs are a convenient protein source for vegetarians, together with meals that combine higher protein sources like tofu, lentils, mixed beans, nuts, and seeds, is the best approach.

What is the main problem with veganism?

Not everyone has the capability to follow a vegan diet and you must follow it for the right reasons, not just to lose weight. Some packaged foods will have ingredients unsuitable for vegans, but adopting a diet that focuses on natural and fresh produce makes it much easier to control.

Can you be vegan and healthy?

Yes, you can be vegan and healthy. But, there needs to be proper planning and implementation when you are on a vegan diet to avoid any nutrient deficiencies which may require supplementing.

What are the risks of a plant-based diet?

There is a risk of inadequate protein, vitamin, and mineral intake when you are on a vegan diet. But, you can overcome this risk with proper planning by choosing the right food to eat and any necessary supplements, such as vitamin B12, iron, zinc, calcium, and iodine.

Can you be strong without eating meat?

Yes, you can avoid meat and still be strong. To be strong, you need protein together with regular exercise. There are plenty of foods to get your protein from like tofu, beans, and lentils.

Is a plant-based diet healthier?

If following a plant-based diet helps you eat a more balanced range of high-quality foods like fruits and vegetables, whole grains and legumes, whilst avoiding nutrient deficiencies, then yes it would be healthier for you. Following this approach and including smaller portions of meat and fish would also be very healthy.

How to build muscle on a vegan/vegetarian diet?

Here are some tips for building muscle on a vegan/vegetarian diet:

1) Do regular strength training

2) Eat high protein plant foods

3) Include these foods with every meal and snack

4) Sleep for a minimum of 7-8 hours each night

5) Include a soy or pea protein supplement to increase your protein intake

6) Supplement with creatine monohydrate

Is vegetarianism better than veganism?

Vegetarian diets have a greater range of foods they can eat making it easier to enjoy a variety of foods to get enough protein and prevent nutrient deficiencies. Vegan diets are not necessarily healthier than vegetarian diets because of their limited food options, but one person's vegan diet may be healthier than another person's vegetarian diet if they are eating more fruit and vegetables, whole grains, and preventing nutrient deficiencies.

How common is a calcium deficiency in vegans and vegetarians?

Calcium deficiency is common among vegans. Most vegans lack enough calcium because they struggle to replace dairy foods in their diet, and therefore need to take a calcium supplement to prevent osteoporosis later in their life. Since vegetarians eat dairy products, they should have no problem with calcium deficiency

Do vegetarians face iodine deficiency problems?

Iodine intake for vegetarians is low as they don't eat fish, but they can get it from dairy sources like yogurt and milk. Seaweed is high in iodine which is suitable for vegans and vegetarians, otherwise, a supplement may be required.

The above information is reprinted with kind permission from Webber Nutrition.
© 2023 Webber Nutrition

www.webber-nutrition.co.uk

Plant-based protein

Protein is essential for the growth and repair of our cells and tissues. Although protein is often associated with animal products, many plant foods are also good sources. As long as protein comes from a variety of plant sources, vegans and vegetarians can easily meet their protein needs. In this infographic we show the protein content of different vegan and vegetarian dishes rich in plant based protein.

How many grams of protein per portion of different plant-based proteins?

9.5g
Wholewheat pasta 75g

9.7g
Red lentils 120g

Lentil spaghetti 'bolognese'
19.2 g protein

4.5g
Pistachio 25g

5g
Sunflower seeds 25g

10.4g
Quinoa 75g

Quinoa & pistachio salad
19.9g protein

5.9g
Whole grain wrap 65g

10.7g
Pinto beans 120

5.8g
Brown rice 75

Bean burrito
22.4 g protein

14g
Soya beans 120g

4.4g
Cashews 25g

Soya bean masala
18.8g protein

24.8g
Seitan 100g

Plant-based BBQ
24.8g protein

8.1-11g
Tofu 100g

8.3g
Millet 75g

10.3g
Red kidney beans 120g

6.1g
Pumpkin seeds 25g

Poké bowl
32.8 g protein

8.5
Baked beans 120

4.7
Whole grain Bread 40

20.7
Tempeh 100

Cooked breakfast
33.9 g protein

4.1g
Chia seeds 25g

5.3g
Almonds 25g

5.5g
Rolled oats 50g

6.2g
Soy drink 200ml

Porridge
21.1 g protein

7g
Butter bean 120g

8.5g
Chickpeas 120g

4.6g
Sesame seeds (Tahini) 25g

Hummus & greek gigantes beans
20.1 g protein

eufic.org

Source: EUFIC - values calculated using data from the uk and dutch food composition databases

A diet consisting mainly of fruit is bad for you

An article from The Conversation.

By James Brown, Associate Professor in Biology and Biomedical Science, Aston University

Plant-based diets have become increasingly popular in recent years, both for health and ethical reasons. One extreme form of plant-based diet is 'fruitarianism', a diet based largely on consumption of raw fruit. At first glance, this may sound healthy, but what effect will this type of restrictive diet have on the body? And is it a healthy diet choice?

There is solid evidence that plant-based diets are good for the body. Plant-based diets may reduce the risk of heart disease by 40% and stroke by 29%. Plant-based diets have also been shown to be a useful strategy for helping people lose weight.

While plant-based diets have clear benefits for health and environmental sustainability, fruitarianism is one of the most restrictive diet choices available and has almost no evidence to support health benefits. There is no definitive description of what a fruitarian diet should consist of, although one commonly cited 'rule' is that between 55% and 75% of the diet should comprise raw fruit. Beyond this, there is some variability; some fruitarians eat grains, some also eat nuts and oils.

Apple co-founder, Steve Jobs, experimented with a fruitarian diet, supplementing it with nuts, seeds and grains. Some adherents of fruitarianism stick to an 80-10-10 rule: 80% of calories coming from fresh fruit and vegetables, 10% coming from protein and 10% from fat. This rule is mistakenly based on the belief that humans are not omnivores, but 'frugivores' – animals that prefer to eat raw fruit. Proponents of this belief state that the human digestive system is physiologically designed to digest fruit and raw vegetables. While this may have once been true, the human body has evolved.

Some fruitarians claim that 'going raw' has had marked benefits including curing cancer and eliminating bloating and body odour. There is no robust evidence to back up these claims.

The idea of consuming a fruit-only (or fruit-heavy) diet might appear a healthy option at first glance, but there are potentially many problems with this form of restrictive eating.

There are clear and significant physical health issues to consider when the human body is provided with a largely fruit-based diet. Following this eating pattern excludes essential food groups and nutrients that the body needs to maintain normal health.

While most fruit is considered to be healthy and nutritious, a diet that almost solely relies on fruits will be deficient in nutrients, including protein, iron, calcium, vitamin B (including vitamin B12) and D, zinc and omega-3 fatty acids. Deficiency in these nutrients can have significant health implications including rickets and osteomalacia (a softening of the bones), anaemia and issues with bones, muscles and skin. Put simply, fruit does not contain all the nutrients the body needs.

In addition to what is missing in a fruitarian diet, the high levels of fructose have to be considered. Fructose is a simple sugar, like glucose, but the human body processes it very differently. Fructose is metabolised solely in the liver. Excess fructose consumption can cause fat buildup in the liver, leading to insulin resistance in the liver and non-alcoholic fatty liver disease. While there is controversy as to whether fructose from fruit is as bad as fructose syrup, which is added to foods to sweeten them, experiments in rats fed a high fructose diet showed similarities to human fatty liver disease.

Serious harm

Beyond the potential physical effects of fruitarianism, restrictive diets are also often associated with an eating disorder known as orthorexia nervosa, or an unhealthy obsession with eating 'pure' food only. This means that what can start off as a healthy move towards eating more fruit and vegetables and less junk food can lead to an eating disorder, depression and anxiety.

Worryingly, isolated cases of death or significant disease have been reported when a fruitarian style diet has been followed. Examples include a nine-month-old girl dying after being fed a fruit-only diet. The girl died vastly underweight and malnourished. Additionally, a 49-year-old man was recently reported to have developed reversible dementia after subsisting on a fruit-only diet.

With little evidence of the benefits of such a restrictive diet, it is clear that people who follow this restrictive diet are potentially putting their health at serious risk. Supplementation with foods that provide the missing nutrients may help, but may be rejected by some with orthodox views on fruitarianism. Before changing a diet, especially if the change is going to be extreme, it is always wise to speak to your doctor first. Incorporating more fruit and vegetables as part of a balanced diet is a far safer, healthier way to approach fruit consumption.

25 August 2021

Perfect storm: understanding why plant-based is suddenly under attack

By Jim Manson

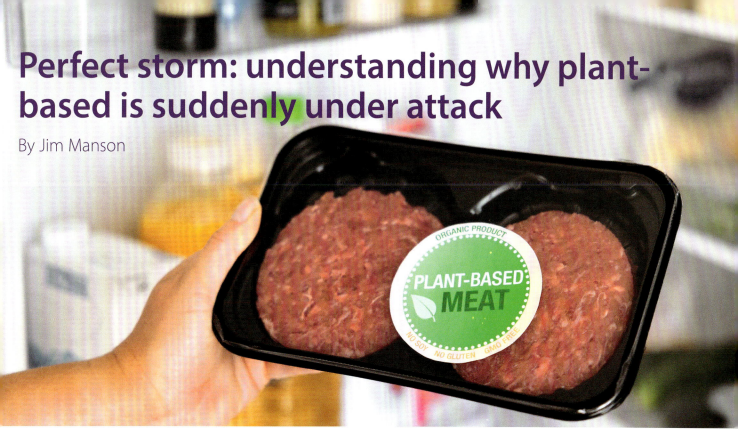

The explosive growth of the plant-based food sector is creating the biggest disruption to the food industry in half a century. The figures alone are dizzying. According to a new report by Bloomberg Intelligence the global plant-based market will grow from US$30 billion in 2021 to a staggering US$160 billion by 2030. But the influence and reach of the plant-based food industry goes well beyond market building.

Plant-based food sector is a cornerstone to the 'green transition'

Lauded by environmentalists and public health experts alike, this agile and innovative growth industry is seen by many as offering the best chance we have to wean populations away from the ecologically destructive food systems responsible for a global epidemic of chronic disease. As a result, plant-based sits at the heart of major food policy initiatives such as the EAT-Lancet Planetary Health Diet and the FAO's Common Vision for Sustainable Food. A switch to plant-based proteins is also a cornerstone to the 'green transition' called for by the European Green Deal.

Until recently, 'buy-in' to plant-based solutions to the global climate and health crises appeared so complete that questioning them was almost unthinkable. But, suddenly, plant-based is coming under attack – and some of the loudest criticism is coming from within the natural and organic movement.

Techno fixes

Long-term organic supporter and campaigner against factory farming Joanna Blythman warns of 'a rise of righteous and vituperative plant-food evangelism'. Former Ecologist editor and anti-GM activist Pat Thomas claims that, that 'vested interests, billionaire-owned think tanks and large corporations' are taking ownership of the plant-based food movement to 'continue to hijack the sustainability agenda'.

More widely, the natural food sector worries that a plant-based hegemony is emerging, that prioritises 'techno-fixes' over more traditional forms of agriculture and ways of eating.

What's happening here? Why are natural allies now at loggerheads over a food category that has been a staple of the health food movement for decades?

To answer that question, we need to put the modern plant-based food industry into context. Vegetarianism has been a core 'health food' offering for as long as the health food industry has existed (well over a century). Veganism, a term coined in the 1940s, is a slightly newer addition to the mix. Vegetarian and vegan foods were also a staple of the more recent natural food scene, where their ethical and health benefits were seen as a good fit with organic and whole food principles. The fact that some early vegan products – the ubiquitous 'texturised vegetable protein' (TVP), for example – were highly processed, was quietly accommodated. The products were mostly generic, and the specialist vegan brands that existed were small players, often independently owned.

Perfect storm

Fast-forward to the 2020s and we see something very different. Today plant-based (the term that is now the dominant descriptor) is a food industry mega-trend, attracting astonishing levels of investment from multinational food businesses and private equity firms.

The climate crisis, health and animal welfare concerns – all amplified by the global pandemic – have combined to create a perfect storm for the plant-based food industry. And all of this is happening at exactly the same time that a food biotechnology revolution is taking place. The result: one enormous global market opportunity.

While a new generation of environment, health and ethics-focused start-ups lead on awareness-building – inspiring swathes of new vegan and plant-based diet followers – the fear is that multinational food brands are quickly taking control of the plant-based agenda.

The criticism of the plant-based food industry that has broken out recently tends to focus on three main areas: the perceived 'corporate take-over' of the sector, just mentioned; nutritional and health issues; and ecological impacts.

> ### 'While a new generation of environment, health and ethics-focused start-ups lead on awareness-building, the fear is that multinational food brands are quickly taking control of the plant-based agenda'

Following the money

It is partly the rate at which money is being poured into the plant-based industry that is provoking concern (in 2020 alone US$2.2 billion was invested in the plant based space, half of all the capital investment in the industry since 1980). But the biggest concern is who is making the investment. As well as private equity firms, much of the money coming into the sector is from food industry multinationals and retailers – Nestlé, Danone, McDonalds and Starbuck's, Unilever (offering over 700 vegan products in Europe) and Cargill among them.

With the bulk of investment money coming from big business, the plant-based food sector is shifting firmly in the direction of industrialised production and scalable technologies. As *New Nutrition Journal* editor Julian Melletin recently put it: 'I get the impression that if you turned up to the private equity people with a business plan saying "I'm going to produce a highly processed, multi ingredient meat substitute" they'd throw money at you because they believe that is competitive advantage. If I say "I'm just going make a burger made from plants, nuts, seeds" – they're not interested.'

Health halo

Critics of this trend warn that what is going on is a re-badging of the ultra-processed food industry, with the term 'plant-based' conferring a convenient health halo. As the Belgian food policy expert Frédéric Leroy, comments: 'The megaliths of the agricultural industry have stepped in, realising that the plant-based lifestyle generates large profit margins, by adding value to cheap raw materials such as protein extracts, starches and oils.'

Leroy is one many to claim that self-interest lies behind the very public backing from food multinationals for global initiatives advocating a planetary shift to a plant-based diet. He accuses these firms of 'hiding behind the grandest talk of "ethical" diets and planetary sustainability'.

When Impossible Foods, one of the best known plant-based food companies in the world, exhibited its GMO-derived Impossible Burger at the Natural Products Expo West event in the United States there was an outcry from

the natural products community. The biggest concern was that a product manufactured using genetic engineering techniques was being exhibited at a trade show for 'natural' food. But the incident also highlights the plant-based industry drift towards the techno fix approach, and how that, in turn, attracts more investment (last year, funding of Impossible Foods stood at $1.5 billion).

Dr Robert Verkerk, scientific director of the Alliance for Natural Health International, warns that if 'Big Ag' takes control of the plant-based agenda it will seize the opportunity to perpetuate environmentally destructive intensive mono-cropping. He argues that how we eat is as important as what eat: 'We should be eating foods from regenerative agricultural systems, minimising or avoiding their processing, eating them fresh, fermented in a timely manner, not crucifying them with excess heat, so generating carcinogens'.

Vegan junk food

Joanna Blythman also questions the health arguments made for plant-based foods, if the majority are ultra-processed. She argues that the big vegan revolution does nothing to offset the 'obesogenic' environment. 'Vegan junk food is becoming ever more commonplace, piled full of sugars, or mechanically refined carbs,' she claims.

'We should be eating foods from regenerative agricultural systems, minimising or avoiding their processing'

Meanwhile, groups such as the Sustainable Food Trust (SFT) – led by organic farmer Patrick Holden, say that the environmental case for a global switch to a plant-based diet is simplistic, and often reduced to a 'plant-based good, meat and dairy bad' mantra. SFT argues that, in many parts of Europe, there is now a 'dependence on imported protein, which is produced at a high environment cost'. It has argued, controversially, that 'vegans and others would do better to switch to milk from cows, and especially cows traditionally grazed on grass, if they want to help make a more sustainable planet'. International animal welfare group Compassion in World Farming also favours 'restoring animals to pasture in well-managed, mixed rotational land' over 'chasing high-tech alternative solutions'.

There are warnings too that current plant-based focused policies fail to recognise the needs of emerging nations, and risk disadvantaging small-scale, traditional farming.

A lot of criticism, but is it all fair?

The charge sheet, then, is a long one. But is all of this criticism fair and valid? Is it not, in part, an attempt to protect practises that many independent climate scientists say are accelerating climate change? Is it naive to think that changing food and farming systems on the scale that is going to be needed can be done without the involvement of big business?

Earlier this year *Vegconomist* posed these very questions in an article titled *'Large multinationals are conquering the vegan market. Good or bad thing?'*. Paula González Carracedo, founder and CEO of Madrid-based The Vegan Agency, told the vegan business magazine that her opinion on the subject was 'divided between heart and head'. She explained: 'The pragmatic part tells me that it is good news that the same companies responsible for the decline of the planet and the death of so many millions of animals are taking steps towards veganism and a better world for all.' She believes the involvement of big brands helps 'democratise plant-based's reach', but says she is also 'very concerned about the type of food quality' these companies will offer, and worries about their record on labour inequalities and the environment. Cristina Rodrigo, country manager of ProVeg International in Spain, argues that switching globally to food systems that are more sustainable, resilient and functional will be 'impossible without asking companies and organisations to review and improve their approach'. She adds: 'We have to bring companies like Nestlé and Unilever into this change, regardless of their history'.

It seems unlikely that these two very differing views of the plant-based food industry can be reconciled easily. And this illustrates the tensions that sometimes exist inside the natural and organic space.

Plant-based diet VS plant-based food

Finally, there is another issue that rarely gets the attention it deserves – the important difference between a plant-based diet and plant-based food. When Michael Pollan summarised the advice in his book *Food Rules* as 'eat food, not too much, mostly plants' he really was talking about plants, not the 'edible food-like substances (favoured by) the food-industrial complex'. To underline the point, in Food Rule 19, Pollan writes: 'If it's a plant, eat it. If it was made in a plant, don't'. That too may be an oversimplification (and difficult to achieve in the real world), but it is a health message that we shouldn't ignore.

10 November 2021

Key Fact

- According to a new report by Bloomberg Intelligence the global plant-based market will grow from US $30 billion in 2021 to a staggering US $160 billion by 2030.

Research

Visit a supermarket and compare the nutritional value of a substitute/plant-based meat product with an equivalent meat product - e.g pork sausages with quorn or soya sausages. Look at the protein, salt, fat and fibre content. Which is the healthiest over all?

www.bioecoactual.com

Flexitarian: an adaptable diet for a sustainable future

In our 'Article of the Term' for Spring 2022, Valli Tirounavoucarassou gives us an introduction to being flexitarian, a sustainable diet for those who don't want to ditch meat completely!

By Valli Tirounavoucarassou

As many people discuss what is happening to the climate, it's a difficult question to answer. Our planet is burdened by rising oceans, growing deserts, declining biodiversity, and increasing temperatures. Food production accounts for approximately a quarter of worldwide greenhouse gas emissions meaning preventing global warming is unachievable without dramatic changes to our diets. Meanwhile climate change is simultaneously threatening the global food supply with land and water being overused at an 'exceptional' rate. Laura Wellesley, a senior research fellow in the Environment and Society Programme at Chatham House, says that it is impossible for the world to reach its Paris Agreement targets to reduce global temperature rise to 1.5 °C unless substantial change is made to diets around the world.

Would you believe me if I tell you that simply changing our eating habits could change our life for the better? You might be thinking, 'Oh, not another vegan campaign, please!', but rest assured, this is not about veganism. This is something more flexible, easier to transition to and maintain.

'Are you certain?', you may say. Ladies and gentlemen, please allow me to introduce you to the excellent flexitariandiet, helping build a sustainable future for both you and our beloved planet.

Have you ever considered being a flexitarian? It simply means 'flexible vegetarian'. If the notion of turning vegan or completely vegetarian is too much for you, you may consider flexitarianism, one of the newest eating 'trends'. According to YouGov research, 14% of British people identify as flexitarian. This is more than double the amount of people who claim to eat a vegan, vegetarian, or pescetarian diet.

The term 'flexitarian' became popular in 2008 when registered dietitian Dawn Jackson Blatner released her book: 'The Flexitarian Diet: The Mostly Vegetarian Way to Lose Weight, Be Healthier, Prevent Disease, and Add Years to Your Life'. Flexitarianism is a plant-based diet that claims to reduce your carbon footprint and enhance your health by eating largely vegetarian, plant-derived food while also allowing for the occasional meat eating.

The emergence of the flexitarian diet is a consequence of individuals embracing more environmentally sustainable attitudes to what they eat by limiting meat intake in favor of other protein sources. The Flexitarian Diet has no hard and fast guidelines or suggested calorie and macronutrient amounts. In fact, it is more of a way of life than a diet.

Here are the simple ideals of a flexitarian diet:

- Consume a lot of fruits, veggies, legumes, and whole grains.
- Prioritise plant protein instead of animal protein.
- Be adaptable to occasionally include meat and animal products
- Consume foods that have been minimally processed and are as close to their natural state as possible
- Reduce your intake of sweets and food with added sugar

The Flexitarian Diet is the best choice for those trying to eat healthy because of its adaptability and focus on what to include instead of what to exclude. Dawn Jackson Blatner's aforementioned book explains how to begin eating flexitarian by consuming specified amounts of meat every week. Following her precise advice, however, is not essential to begin eating flexitarian. Some people who adhere to the diet may consume more meat products than others. The overall objective is to consume more healthy plant foods and less meat.

Interested in the concept? Discover the primary advantages of a flexitarian diet in the sections below.

How frequently do flexitarians consume meat?

There is no specific amount of meat that a flexitarian can consume; it is entirely up to the person. However, Dawn Jackson Blatner's book recommends a limit of 28 ounces of lean meat each week. Better yet, consume three ounces of lean meat three times each week.

What kinds of meat can you consume?

Remember that the flexitarian diet's ultimate objective is to consume more healthy plant-based foods and less meat. When it comes to protein, the majority of your protein should come from plants rather than animals.

This can contain beef, chicken, fish, shrimp, crab, lamb, and any other low-fat item. When you do consume meat, pick organic, free-range, pasture-raised sources or grass-fed beef, chicken, or turkey. Also, consider slimmer cuts to reduce excess animal fat. Due to the flexitarian diet not being strictly vegan or vegetarian, you can choose whether or not to include fish; just be sure to select those caught in the wild.

Do flexitarians consume dairy?

Yes! Flexitarians can consume both plant-based and animal-derived dairy products in moderation. The majority of the dairy in flexitarian meals is in the form of milk, yogurt, and modest amounts of lower-fat cheeses like feta, parmesan, and ricotta.

Will you get enough nutrients?

Vitamin B12, calcium, iron, and zinc are the most often deficient nutrients in vegan or vegetarian diets. Plant proteins are insufficient, so vegans who adhere to strict veganism must take dietary supplements. Those who avoid all meat may be lacking in protein, vitamin D3, DHA, and iron.

Vitamin B12 is exclusively present in animal foods and is required for the formation of red blood cells and DNA.

250ml of milk contains around half of the recommended daily amount of B12. Around 30% of the calcium in milk is absorbed by the body, but calcium- rich plant-based milk has large amounts of oxalate and phytates which inhibit calcium absorption. One scoop of whey protein isolate contains 68 percent of your daily zinc requirement. Plant proteins are not sufficient; therefore, ingesting complementary plant proteins to obtain all of the necessary amino acids required by the body can be difficult, especially for pregnant women and elderly people.

Individuals who adopt flexitarian diets can receive all their necessary nutrients by consuming animal-derived foods on occasion, therefore maintaining their health.

What are the merits of adopting a flexitarian lifestyle?

Many research studies have found that flexitarian or semi-vegetarian diets may also have potential health advantages, with the greatest evidence pointing to weight loss and metabolic health benefits, such as lower diabetes risk and lower blood pressure. Eating more plant-based foods will also increase the demand for additional land to be dedicated to cultivating fruits and vegetables for human consumption rather than cattle feed. Plant cultivation uses significantly fewer resources than raising animals for food.

What do climate statistics have to say about adopting a flexitarian diet?

Animal derived food products (from cattle, in particular) are the principal source of methane emissions. Over a 20-year period, methane is 86 times more powerful than carbon dioxide as a greenhouse gas. Therefore, by lowering your meat consumption, you are directly contributing to a campaign to help protect the world. Initially, you could eliminate meat from one meal every day before reducing meat consumption to once or twice a week. Every small step makes a big difference, with studies showing that transitioning from the Western diet with meat in nearly every meal to a flexitarian diet can reduce gas emissions by 7%.

According to a study published in the scientific journal called Nature, switching to a more plant-based, flexitarian diet could cut greenhouse gas emissions by up to 52% compared to baseline forecasts for 2050.

If everyone began eating less meat, the negative environmental impacts stemming from intensive animal farming would be reduced or even eliminated. Eating more sustainably sourced meat may even have less environmental impact than coffee or cocoa bean consumption which emit greenhouse gases due to deforestation used to clear land for farming.

Where to start?

If you've tried and failed to give up meat or dairy, you're not alone! According to research, 84 percent of vegans and vegetarians eventually switch back to meat, with 53 percent quitting after just one year. That is why adopting a flexitarian diet is an excellent place to start.

According to Blatner, new flexitarians should start simple: attempt two meat-free days per week and eight small amounts of meat dispersed across the rest of your meals. Work your way up to five meat-free days and three small pieces each week. Even if you can only avoid one red meat meal each week, it's preferable over doing nothing. According to the Committee on Climate Change guidelines, a 20% reduction in beef, lamb, and dairy consumption would help the UK reduce greenhouse gas emissions to near zero by 2050, giving you a target to contribute towards.

If this is still too much, small pledges like Meat-Free Mondays are a great approach to start reducing the effect of your diet on animals, the environment, and your health. Focusing on plant-based cuisine and eating less meat might be difficult for some people. To begin, you can buy fantastic bean-based burgers, canned bean and lentil soup, and bean-based pastas. Once you are more comfortable, it's much better to prepare your own home-made versions. Don't be frightened to try anything new with this diet!

9 March 2022

About The Author: Valli Tirounavoucarassou is a WILD Food & Drink contributor who is now pursuing a Master's degree in Sustainable Food Systems at the Swedish University of Agricultural Science in Sweden. Her research expertise entails producing climate-smart and resource-efficient food products. Considering herself a flexitarian; she works on a sustainable way of life with a focus on the food system. You can find her on Linkedin.

www.wildmag.co.uk

Body less able to absorb protein from vegan 'meat', study suggests

Findings may lead to development of ingredients to increase uptake of nutrients from plant-based products.

By Vishwan Sankaran

Proteins in plant-based meat alternatives may not be as accessible to human cells as those from real meat, a new study has suggested.

While plants rich in protein, such as soy beans, are commonly used worldwide, researchers, including those from the Ohio State University in the US, say it is unclear how much of the nutrient makes it into human cells.

In the study published on Wednesday in the *Journal of Agricultural and Food Chemistry*, scientists assessed if human cells grown in a lab absorb the same quantities of the protein building blocks peptides from meat alternatives as they do from chicken.

The findings may lead to new ingredients that may increase the uptake of nutrients from plant-based meat products, researchers say.

To mimic the look and texture of real meat, they say plant-based substitutes are usually made by dehydrating plants into a powder and mixing them with seasonings.

These mixtures are then typically heated, moistened, and processed through an extruder to produce plant-based meat, researchers say, adding that these products are often thought to be more nutritious since the plants used to make them are high in protein and low in undesirable fats.

However, researchers say the proteins in substitutes may not break down into peptides as well as those from meats.

In the new study, they analysed the quantity of peptides absorbed from a model meat alternative by human cells and compared this to the amount the cells absorbed from a piece of chicken breast (CB).

For the research, scientists created a model meat alternative (MA) made of soy and wheat gluten with the extrusion process.

When cut open, they say the material had long fibrous pieces inside, just like chicken.

Researchers then cooked pieces of the substitute and chicken meat, and broke them down using an enzyme that humans use to digest food.

They found that peptides and their amino acid building blocks from the meat substitutes were less water-soluble than those from chicken, and were also 'not absorbed as well by human cells'.

'The amino acid composition showed fewer essential and non-essential amino acids in the MA permeate than in the CB permeate,' scientists wrote in the study.

They say future studies can help identify ingredients that can help boost the peptide uptake of plant-based meat substitutes.

24 June 2022

Key Fact

- Amino acids are the building blocks of proteins.

Research

Conduct some online research to find 5 foods that are high in amino acids.

www.independent.co.uk

Vegetarian women more likely to fracture hips in later life, study shows

Research suggests some vegetarians may not get sufficient nutrients for good bone and muscle health.

By Ian Sample, Science Editor

Women who are vegetarian are more likely to experience hip fractures in later life than those who frequently eat meat, a UK study has found.

Researchers analysed health and diet records from more than 26,000 women and found that over a roughly 22-year period, vegetarians were a third more likely to break a hip than those who regularly ate meat.

The reasons for the greater risk are unclear but researchers suspect some vegetarians may not get sufficient nutrients for good bone and muscle health, leaving them prone to falls and fractures.

'The message for vegetarians is don't give up your diet, because it is healthy for other things and environmentally friendly, but do take care to plan well and don't miss out on nutrients that you exclude when you don't eat meat or fish,' said Dr James Webster, a researcher at the University of Leeds.

Vegetarian diets are often considered healthier than meat-containing diets and they can reduce the risk of diabetes, obesity, heart disease and certain cancers. But the study published in BMC Medicine highlights the importance of a balanced diet whatever people eat.

'It's likely that vegetarians, for one reason or another, and potentially because of lower intakes of important nutrients, have weaker bones and lower muscle mass and both of those things predispose people to hip fractures,' Webster said.

About 90% of hip fractures are linked to falls, which are more common in older people, who tend to be more frail and have weaker bones. But fractures can often drive further frailty, which increases the risk of more falls and worse frailty.

The researchers suspect vegetarians are more likely to be underweight than meat eaters, and that beyond having weaker bones and muscles may also have less fat, which can act as a cushion when people fall.

Given the findings, Webster said vegetarians may want to consider eating fortified cereals with added iron and B12 for bone health, and to ensure they are getting enough protein, through foods such as nuts, legumes and beans.

The researchers drew on data from the UK Women's Cohort Study, which is tracking women over time to assess links between diet and health. Records for 26,318 women aged 35 to 69 revealed that 822, or 3%, had hip fractures in a roughly 22-year period. About 28% of the women were vegetarians and 1% were vegans.

The researchers compared the rate of hip fractures in vegetarians, pescatarians – those who eat fish but not meat – and occasional meat eaters with frequent meat eaters. The frequent meat eaters ate meat at least five times a week.

Webster said more work was needed to see if vegetarian men had a similarly greater risk of hip fractures. Previous work suggests vegetarian men and women have poorer bone health on average when compared with meat-eaters 'but risk of hip fracture in male vegetarians still remains unclear', he said.

Eating less meat is one of the most important lifestyle changes people can make to reduce greenhouse gas emissions. Research from Leeds University last year found that non-vegetarian diets created 59% more emissions than vegetarian ones.

In work published in 2020, Dr Tammy Tong, a senior nutritional epidemiologist, and others at the University of Oxford, found that compared with meat eaters, vegetarians had a 25% greater risk of hip fractures, with the risk even higher for vegans at 31%.

Vegetarians in the Leeds study had a lower body mass index (BMI) than regular-meat eaters, lower protein intake and lower vitamin D intake, 'all of which are potential risk factors for hip fracture,' she said.

'Vegetarians should pay particular attention to maintaining a healthy body weight, and making sure that they have an adequate intake of protein and other nutrients important for bone health, including calcium and vitamin D.'

11 August 2022

www.theguardian.com

In the news: Is a vegetarian diet linked to hip fractures?

Recent news stories reported that women who follow a vegetarian diet are more likely to suffer hip fractures than those who eat meat, suggesting nutritional deficiencies and lower body mass index (BMI) as possible causes. Meatless diets are becoming increasingly popular in Western countries, possibly due to increasing evidence of reduced risks of several chronic diseases and a lower environmental footprint of vegetarian diets compared to omnivorous diets. So, should you really abandon a vegetarian diet according to these new findings? Here are a few things to keep in mind when reading the headlines.

The study behind the headlines

The study behind the news was carried out by researchers from the University of Leeds in the UK with the aim to investigate the risk of hip fracture in occasional meat-eaters, pescatarians and vegetarians compared to regular meat-eaters in middle-aged UK women, as well as to determine if potential associations between each diet group and hip fracture risk differ across levels of BMI.[1]

The current study used health and lifestyle data from the UK Women's Cohort Study, which is a large long-term study involving 500,000 women (aged 35-69 years) from England, Scotland and Wales aimed at exploring the links between diet and chronic disease. The study started during the 1990s with participants filling in a so-called food frequency questionnaire (FFQ) about their usual eating habits over the past year. Based on their responses, women were classed as regular meat eaters (≥5 times per week), occasional meat eaters (<5 times per week), pescatarian (ate fish but no meat) and vegetarian or vegan (ate neither meat nor fish). The researchers then followed these participants up over a period of, on average, 22 years, and combined data from hospital records to identify cases of hip fracture.

After the follow-up period had passed, the researchers analysed the data from 26,318 women who had complete data. They found that vegetarians and vegans, but not occasional meat eaters or pescatarians, had a 33% higher risk of hip fracture compared with the regular meat eater group. Within this association, the study has considered multiple factors such as ethnicity, smoking status, level of physical activity, menopausal status, reproductive history and other diseases that could potentially influence the hip fracture outcome. Further analysis considering BMI, specific vitamins and minerals (e.g., calcium and vitamin D) or dietary fatty acids found that none of these factors made a meaningful difference to the results.

The researchers suggest that future exploration of other factors (e.g., supplemental sources of specific nutrients and circulating vitamin D concentrations) beyond BMI and nutrient intakes could shed light on the observed associations. Besides, further research is needed to look at the link in other population groups, such as men and non-European populations.

What to keep in mind when reading the study's conclusions?

The study does not prove that vegetarian diets are the cause of hip fracture.

Despite careful attempts to account for multiple health and lifestyle factors such as ethnicity, smoking status, level of physical activity etc., that could potentially influence the hip fracture outcome, observational studies such as this, cannot prove direct cause and effect. Furthermore, other unmeasured dietary or lifestyle factors may be involved in the intricate link with hip fractures. Besides, self-administered questionnaire responses from the FFQ may introduce inaccuracies and it is difficult to ensure that they fully reflect a person's health, lifestyle and long-term dietary patterns.

There was no clear evidence that low BMI or nutrient deficiencies provide the answer.

Media reports and the accompanying press release discuss lower BMI or nutritional deficiencies as potential explanations for the observed results. However, it is important to highlight that the study thoroughly explored the individual effect of such factors, with none having a significant impact on the results (i.e., the higher risk of hip fracture in vegetarians was not explained by any dietary nutrient intake nor entirely by BMI). Despite previous research showing an established association between osteoporosis (a condition which predisposes to fracture) and lower BMI or low calcium intake, for example, this specific study does not provide such evidence.

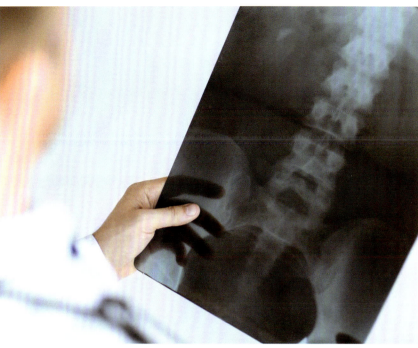

The results might not be applicable to current populations.

The popularity of vegetarian and vegan diets and food availability has increased considerably over the past 20 years. Therefore, food and nutrient intakes in vegetarians in recent years could differ from the periods in which data were collected. As a result, the outcomes cannot be completely generalised to modern-day vegetarians. Also, as the authors acknowledge, neither can the findings be applied to non-white, non-European populations or to men. Moreover, vegetarians and vegans could not be analysed separately due to few study participants, including only 130 vegans (0.5% of women), 5 of whom developed hip fractures.

The wider benefits of a high fruit and vegetable intake were not explored.

Despite some media outlets reporting that 'being vegetarian might be bad for your health later in life' the study has only looked at the link between being a vegetarian and hip fracture. It does not explore the various health benefits associated with a diet high in fruit and vegetables, nor conversely, the adverse effects that have been associated with a diet high in red and processed meat. As such, any small increased risk of hip fracture – if a true link – may be outweighed by the positive effects of adopting a vegetarian diet.

What do authorities say?

- The European osteoporosis guidelines (2019) list risk factors for fracture probability. These include, for example, gender, low BMI, prior fragility fracture, parental history of hip fracture, steroid treatment, current smoking and alcohol intake. For lifestyle prevention they advise regular weight-bearing exercise and ensuring adequate daily calcium intake (800-1200 mg), dietary protein and vitamin D (800 IU or 20 mcg for postmenopausal women), using supplements if necessary. The guidance makes no mention of specific dietary patterns, such as vegetarian or vegan diets.[2]

- In 2021 the WHO published a report on the health impact of plant-based diets (including vegetarian and vegan diets). Overall, they recommend a predominantly plant-based diet low in salt, saturated fats and added sugars as part of a healthy lifestyle. They state that such diets lower the risk of early mortality and protect against chronic diseases, supporting the evidence that high red and processed meat is associated with risk of chronic disease. However, WHO highlights that strict vegan diets raise concerns about nutrient deficiencies, including vitamins D and B12 and calcium.[3]

- EUFIC also provides a summary (2021) on plant-based diets, their health and environmental benefits, emphasising that transitioning to a plant-based diet should focus on increasing healthy plant foods and be less concerned with reducing animal products. It also highlights that plant-based diets can still be unhealthy if high in fat, sugar and salt, and that particular care is needed if following a vegan diet to ensure adequate nutrition.

References

1. Webster, J., Greenwood, D. C., & Cade, J. E. (2022). Risk of hip fracture in meat-eaters, pescatarians, and vegetarians: results from the UK Women's Cohort Study. BMC medicine, 20(1), 1-10.

2. Kanis, J. A., Cooper, C., Rizzoli, R., & Reginster, J. Y. (2019). European guidance for the diagnosis and management of osteoporosis in postmenopausal women. Osteoporosis International, 30(1), 3-44.

3. World Health Organization. (2021). Plant-based diets and their impact on health, sustainability and the environment: a review of the evidence: WHO European Office for the Prevention and Control of Noncommunicable Diseases. Copenhagen: WHO Regional Office for Europe.

Last updated: 24 August 2022

eufic

www.eufic.org

Raw vegan diet may be a risk to your health – here's why

An article from The Conversation.

By Laura Brown, Senior Lecturer in Nutrition, Food, and Health Sciences, Teesside University

Vegan diets have become increasingly popular over the years, especially among people looking to improve their health. Indeed, a growing body of evidence shows that plant-based diets (including vegan diets) can have many benefits for health, and have been linked to lower heart disease risk alongside decreased body weight and cholesterol levels.

However, some people are taking the vegan diet to the extreme, choosing only to eat raw plant foods that can be consumed without any cooking. Some also exclude foods that have been changed from their natural form or processed (such as oat or almond milk).

Proponents of this diet claim that cooking causes ingredients to lose some of their important nutrients and enzymes. By consuming raw plant foods, they believe the diet will improve energy levels, prevent (and even reverse) disease and improve overall health.

But research suggests that raw vegan diets, if followed for a long time, may cause more harm than good. Here's why:

You may miss out on important nutrients

Research does suggest that some raw foods may be healthier than cooked foods. For example, cooking causes brussels sprouts and red cabbage to lose as much as 22% of their thiamine content. This is a form of vitamin B1 which keeps the nervous system healthy.

Though some vegetables may lose nutrients during cooking, others have a greater nutrient content when cooked. This is because some nutrients are bound within the cell walls of the vegetables. Cooking breaks the cell walls down, allowing the nutrients to be released and more readily absorbed by the body.

For example, when spinach is cooked, it becomes easier for the body to absorb the calcium is contains. Research has also found that while cooking tomatoes reduces their vitamin C content by 28%, it increases their lycopene content by more than 50%. Lycopene has been associated with a lower risk of a range of chronic diseases including cardiovascular disease, cancer and heart disease. Asparagus, mushrooms, carrots, broccoli, kale and cauliflower are other examples of vegetables that are more nutrient-dense when cooked.

Cooked vegetables can also supply the body with more antioxidants. These are molecules that can fight against a type of harmful molecule known as free radicals, which can damage cells and may lead to disease over time. Some vegetables (including asparagus, mushrooms, spinach, tomatoes and broccoli) contain higher levels of the antioxidants beta-carotene (which the body turns into vitamin A), lutein and lycopene when cooked than they do when raw.

Vitamin and mineral deficiencies are likely

Raw vegan diets are likely to lack many important vitamins and minerals – namely vitamins B12 and D, selenium, zinc, iron and two types of omega-3 fatty acids. This is because many of the foods that contain high levels of these vitamins and minerals come from animals – such as meat and eggs. These vitamins all play a key role in the structure, development and production of brain and nerve cells, alongside supporting a healthy immune system.

Of particular concern are vitamin B12 levels. A study on people who followed strict raw food diets found that 38% of participants were deficient in vitamin B12. This is concerning, especially given vitamin B12 deficiency is associated with a range of problems, including jaundice, mouth ulcers, vision problems, depression and other mood changes.

The same study also found that a strict, raw vegan diet increased levels of homocysteine (an amino acid broken down by vitamin B12) because of B12 deficiency. This is a concern as increased homocysteine levels can potentially increase the risk of cardiovascular disease and stroke.

May lead to loss of periods

If not planned correctly, the raw vegan diet may lead to unintentional weight loss if you aren't consuming the amount of calories your body needs to function. This is particularly concerning for young women.

Researchers have found that 30% of women under 45 who followed a raw food diet for more than three years had partial to complete amenorrhea (absence of menstruation). This is likely because of weight loss caused by the raw vegan diet. Amenorrhea can cause a range of issues, including infertility, as well as reduced bone mineral density and osteoporosis. Other studies have also shown that young women who consume 22-42% fewer calories than required were at greater risk of suppressed reproductive function.

While following a plant-based diet can have many benefits for health, the raw vegan diet may potentially be taking things a bit too far and may come with even greater risks if not followed carefully. If you are planning to do a raw vegan diet, it's important to plan carefully to ensure you are consuming all the nutrients you need for optimal health, in the required amounts. I also wouldn't recommend following it for a long period of time because of the many risks it may have.

2 November 2022

Tofu worse for the environment than meat, say farmers

This is despite studies showing that following a vegan diet could be the 'single biggest way' to reduce your environmental impact.

By Olivia Petter

Meat is often derided as one of the most environmentally damaging foods to consume, but new research is leading some farmers to claim that tofu could actually be worse.

This is despite studies showing that following a vegan diet could be the 'single biggest way' to reduce your environmental impact on earth.

Speaking at the National Farmers Union (NFU) on Monday, Dr Graham McAuliffe of the Rothamsted Institute explained that his unpublished research on tofu has found that the soya-based protein could have a more drastic impact on the planet than beef, pork and chicken.

Dr McAuliffe, who specialises in measuring the environmental impact of foods, pointed out that his findings should be 'interpreted with caution' given they were currently just a 'proof of concept', reports The Times.

'Without a doubt, peas and ground nuts always have a lower environmental impact than any livestock products,' he said.

'But if you look at tofu, which is processed so there is more energy going into its production, when you correct for the fact that the protein in it is not as digestible compared to the meat-based products, you can see that it could actually have a higher global warming potential than any of the monogastric animals.

'To get the same amount of protein, tofu is worse.'

It's not the first time tofu has come under fire for its carbon footprint.

In 2010, a report conducted on behalf of the World Wide Fund (WWF) warned of the dangers of thinking that soya-based products were guaranteed to have low carbon emissions.

It stated: 'Our analysis shows that direct substitution of livestock products in the diet with analogue high protein products based on, for example, soya involves increased dependence on imported crop commodities.

'Such a strategy is likely to increase the total soya intake of the UK food chain.'

Instead, the report advised those looking to substitute meat in their diets to do so 'through a general increase in crop products' such as lentils and chickpeas, which it said was a 'more effective and sustainable strategy' to reduce the carbon footprint of your diet.

Other studies have found that eating a vegan diet could be the 'single biggest way' to reduce your environmental impact on earth.

Researchers at the University of Oxford found in 2018 that cutting meat and dairy products from your diet could reduce an individual's carbon footprint from food by up to 73 per cent.

Meanwhile, if everyone stopped eating these foods, they found that global farmland use could be reduced by 75 per cent, an area equivalent to the size of the US, China, Australia and the EU combined.

Not only would this result in a significant drop in greenhouse gas emissions, it would also free up wild land lost to agriculture, one of the primary causes for mass wildlife extinction.

12 February 2020

Is a plant-based diet best for the environment?

By Mariah Hughes

While there's no doubt a plant-based diet is, overall, better for the environment than a meat-based diet, eating vegan isn't completely flawless.

From exotic fruit and veg that clocks up air miles, to nuts that use eye-watering amounts of water, there's more to being plant-based than just giving up meat and dairy.

This blog will explore all sides of the vegan diet, addressing both the pros and cons of veganism and how to enjoy more environmentally-friendly conscious food.

Why is eating meat bad for the environment?

Despite some criticisms surrounding veganism, it's generally accepted that meat is one of the biggest offenders when it comes to our individual carbon footprints.

The meat industry generates a high level of dangerous greenhouse gases, from methane produced by livestock to the carbon dioxide released during deforestation for farming.

Beef produces the most greenhouse gases. The UN also estimates around 14% of all man-made greenhouse gas emissions come from the livestock industry.

As well as methane from livestock, factories producing milk products also release carbon dioxide and nitrous oxide. With over 270 million dairy cows across the globe, the demand for milk is rising due in part to population growth and the Westernization of diets, which typically contain more milk products.

Is being vegan more eco-friendly?

With the above in mind, it goes without saying that reducing your meat and dairy intake – following a vegan or vegetarian diet – is better for the environment.

Evidence shows more people are beginning to understand the environmental impact, with meat consumption in the UK dropping 17% in the last 10 years.

Eating veggie results in 2.5 times fewer carbon emissions than a meat diet, while eating vegetarian food for a year could save the same amount of emissions as a family taking a small car off the road for 6 months. You'll also be helping to conserve the land we already have: a vegetarian diet requires 2.5 times less the amount of land needed to grow food.

With around 85% of our fisheries being over fished or exploited, going fish-free can help restore our oceans back to their natural balance, too.

However, while there are many benefits for the environment, it's important to remember not all plant-based food is good for the planet. It isn't as simple as meat is bad, fruit and veg are good. In order to truly reduce your carbon emissions and enjoy a greener lifestyle, every food item must be addressed with a level of scrutiny.

'Bad' plant-based foods

Nothing compares to the ethical and environmental impact of meat, fish and dairy. However, not all vegan foods come with a green stamp of approval. Some fruits and vegetables have a devastatingly high carbon footprint, while other plant-based foods use a large amount of the planet's natural resources.

Air transported fruit and veg can generate more greenhouse gas emissions than locally reared poultry meat. When fruits are out of season in the UK, they are imported from elsewhere to meet demand. Strawberries in winter haven't always been the norm, yet we've come to expect them without a second thought.

Despite being a nation of asparagus growers, especially in the north, the UK has to import the green-stalked veg when it's out of season here. A recent study found that asparagus from Peru had the largest environmental impact of any of the 56 vegetables that were analysed, with 5.3kg of carbon dioxide produced for every kilogram of asparagus.

Avocados have recently come under fire in the press, being used as a reason to criticize the vegan diet. The fleshy green fruit uses a lot of water in the growing and harvesting process – a single mature tree in California (where many avocados are grown) needs up to 209 litres during the summer months. In water-stressed environments where avocados are grown, including California, Chile, Mexico and southern Spain, the local environmental impact can be devastating.

With many people giving up meat due to ethical or environmental reasons, faux-meat products are on the rise. These meat substitutes often use mushrooms or Mycoprotein (made from fungi) to replicate the original feel. While they use a fraction of the land compared to beef, lamb or chicken, the carbon dioxide emissions could still be as high as 6.15kg per kilogram.

Likewise, nut milk has become increasingly popular among those looking to reduce their dairy intake. However, almonds and cashews (two of the nuts commonly used in plant-based milk) are some of the most water-intensive large-scale crops on the planet. It's estimated that tree nuts consume 4,134 litres of water for every kg of shelled nut – a staggering amount.

How to eat more environmentally friendly

It's impossible to completely eliminate our environmental impact when it comes to food. Everything we eat comes with a carbon footprint, no matter how small.

However, it's important we make more conscious choices with plant-based alternatives and consider their levels of eco-friendliness.

It's as simple as paying attention to how plant-based foods are grown and transported, opting for locally grown and seasonal products where you can.

Here are some UK seasonal fruits and vegetables to enjoy:

- Winter: Leeks, celeriac, parsnips, purple sprouting broccoli
- Spring: Asparagus, beetroot, spring greens, blackcurrants.

- Summer: Berries, tomatoes, cucumber, sweetcorn.
- Autumn: Apples, pears, cabbage, pumpkin.

Make sure to avoid greenhouse heated fruits and vegetables, or food that has been air imported.

Look for shops that sell locally-sourced food. You'll be doing your bit for the environment and supporting small local businesses at the same time.

The Natural Food Store in Headingly is choc-full of local, organic produce from fruit and veg to cereals, jams, sauces and pies.

Swillington Organic Farm is just east of Leeds and offers organic meat boxes – parcels of seasonal meat delivered straight to your door.

Similarly, The Organic Pantry delivers tasty organic and local produce to homes all across Yorkshire, as well as organic home and beauty products.

By making use of the above businesses and shopping more consciously, you'll be well on your way to reducing the carbon footprint of your diet and ensuring your plant-based foods are as green as they can be.

25 May 2022

Vegetarian diets may be better for the planet – but the Mediterranean diet is the one omnivores will actually adopt

An article from The Conversation.

By Nicole Allenden, PhD Candidate, School of Psychology, University of New England, Amy Lykins Associate Professor in Clinical Psychology, University of New England & Annette Cowie, Principal Research Scientist, Climate

What we eat and how we produce food matters. Food systems are responsible for more than a quarter of the world's greenhouse gas emissions.

We cannot fully tackle the climate crisis without reducing the greenhouse footprint of our food. The issue is only becoming more urgent, as world population climbs alongside hunger stemming from war disruption of food exports. As people get richer and more urbanised, global consumption of meat and dairy products also grows.

Livestock are the main source of our food emissions and the third highest global source of emissions at 14.5%, after energy (35%) and transport (23%).

To cut these emissions, many advocate switching to plant-rich or plant-only diets. But will people who have a longstanding attachment to meat actually choose to switch? Our new research suggests the sweet spot is the Mediterranean diet, which includes some meat while remaining plant rich and healthy.

What's the problem?

Rearing livestock requires large areas of land, as well as inputs of water and feed. More intensive livestock production is linked to biodiversity loss, land degradation, pollution of waterways, increased risk of zoonotic diseases such as COVID-19, and antibiotic resistance.

While methods of cutting livestock emissions are undergoing development, production is only half the story. To have a real impact, we also need to consider the demand side.

Without reducing the overall demand for meat and dairy, it's unlikely livestock emissions will fall fast enough and far enough. In wealthy countries like Australia, we consume meat and dairy at high rates. Reducing these consumption rates could cut greenhouse emissions and reduce other environmental damage.

So which diet should we eat? Clearly, any acceptable diet needs to be nutritionally adequate. While meat provides essential nutrients, too much of it is linked to diseases like cancer. It's important to consider both environmental and health credentials of a diet. We can add animal welfare to this as well, which tends to be worse in intensive livestock production.

We hope by identifying healthy, environmentally sustainable diets with better animal welfare, we can help people make sustainable dietary choices.

What did we find?

We looked at five common plant-rich diets and assessed their impacts on the environment (carbon footprint, land, and water use), human health, and animal welfare. We focused on food production in high-income countries.

The diets we examined were:

- Mediterranean (plant-heavy with small amounts of red meat, moderate amounts of poultry and fish)

- Flexitarian/semi-vegetarian (meat reduction)

- Pescatarian (fish, no other meat)

- Vegetarian (no meat but dairy and eggs OK)

- Vegan (no animal products)

All five of these plant-rich diets had less environmental impact than the omnivore diet, with no-meat diets (vegan and vegetarian) having the least impact.

We have to add the caveat, however, that environmental footprint measures used to compare diets are simplistic and overlook important indirect effects of shifting diets.

Overall, the Mediterranean diet was deemed the healthiest for humans, while the vegan and vegetarian diets had the best outcomes for animal welfare. When we combined all three measures, vegan and vegetarian diets were found to be the most 'sustainable' diets based on reducing our food footprint, staying healthy, and reducing negative impacts on farm animals.

We know which diets are best. But what diet will people actually choose?

There is often a gulf between what we should do in an ideal world and what we actually do. To tackle this, we examined what people are actually willing to eat. Is promoting a vegan or vegetarian diet the most effective way to reduce demand for meat and dairy?

To find out, we asked 253 Australians what they currently eat and which of the five plant-rich diets they were willing to eat.

Australia is a high meat-eating country, so it's not surprising that most of our respondents (71%) identified as omnivores.

It's also no surprise that the diets least likely to be adopted were the vegan and vegetarian diets, as these diets represented a major shift in most people's eating habits.

As a result, it was the Mediterranean diet – which entails a small reduction in meat consumption – which had the highest likelihood of adoption. Combined with its high health benefits and moderate environmental and animal welfare impacts, we identified it as the best diet to promote.

While some of these results may seem intuitive, we believe by combining social, environmental, human health, and animal welfare elements of food consumption, we gain a more complete picture to spot pitfalls as well as realistic solutions.

For instance, it's likely a waste of precious time and resources to promote diets like the vegan diet which, realistically, most people are not willing to eat. Yet despite the evident lack of enthusiasm from people, most research assessing the environmental impact of different diets has favoured vegan and vegetarian diets.

That's why taking a wider view is important. If we actually want to reduce meat and dairy consumption, we must use approaches that have the best chance of working.

In high-income countries like Australia, that means we should promote the Mediterranean diet as the best diet to begin to tackle the demand for emissions-intensive meat and dairy. We need to start at a realistic point to begin to create a more sustainable global food system.

18 July 2022

Dietary Trends

Chapter 2

5 major trends driving the plant-based food market

By Laura Nettle

The plant-based food market is booming. With one-third of UK consumers choosing to actively reduce their meat consumption, the demand for plant-based innovation is growing at a rapid pace.

A recent report by BIS research estimated that the plant-based market will reach $480.43 billion by 2024, with a projected CAGR of 13.82% from 2019 to 2024. Moreover, Nestlé reported that 87% of Americans are now including plant-based protein in their diets. Figures like these suggest the plant-based market is no longer niche; consumers are hungry for meat and dairy alternatives.

According to recent research by Mintel, there are multiple factors driving the growth of plant-based eating. These include concern for the environment, health and wellness, ethics, and diversity in protein sourcing.

So, FoodBev has provided a breakdown of five factors that are contributing to the surge in plant-based purchases

Climate change

Climate awareness is one factor driving consumers to switch to a more plant-based diet. Significant media coverage that demonstrates the impact of meat and dairy production on greenhouse gases and global warming is building such awareness, Deloitte reported.

Mark Hyman MD, author of *Food: What the Heck Should I Eat,* said: 'People are stepping up to the realities of climate change, and factory-farmed meat and the way we grow most of the food in this country is damaging our land, our air, our water, our communities and our bodies.'

A recent study by the Federation of American Societies for Experimental Biology found the production of plant-based meat alternatives to contribute 10x fewer greenhouse emissions than equivalent beef-based products. Evidence such as this is causing a decline in meat and dairy

consumption, but increased demand for companies that demonstrate a positive environmental impact whilst still offering the protein content that can be found in animal-based products.

Some companies are even utilising the by-products of foods and beverages in a bid to reduce the use of plastics, such as Jose Cuervo's sustainable drinking straws and eco-friendly packaging made from banana plants.

Health & ethics

The shift towards plant-based diets has been predominantly driven by consumer concern surrounding health, wellbeing and animal welfare. According to Deloitte, this switch is being fuelled by numerous reports that describe possible links between processed or red meat and cancers.

Another key driver behind this shift is the positive health benefits that accompany plant-based diets, such as meat-alternatives that are considered high in nutrition, able to assist weight management and thus promote better overall health.

Brands can appeal to both vegans and non-vegans by placing emphasis on the 'free-from' attributes of vegan food and drink products in order to relay a wider health and wellness message, as highlighted by Mintel. Examples of this include Dolfin's chocolate coated chickpea snacks, Plamil's 'sugar-free' chocolate range and Englightened's 'better-for-you' dairy-free ice-cream bars.

Taste

In October 2019, The Good Food Institute found taste to be the primary driver of consumer purchases of plant-based products. It is clear that taste and texture are key factors companies in this market should focus on. Although dramatic improvements have been made with regards to taste, texture and the variety of alternatives available, these factors still remain a major barrier to the consumption of plant-based products for many meat eaters. It is clear that further innovation in both meat and dairy substitutes is the key to growth in this market.

Technology advances have enabled plant-based alternatives, such as soy, peas and nuts, to actually taste somewhat like meat or dairy-based products. In particular, plant-based burgers are often considered parallel to meat-based burgers in terms of texture and flavour, whilst being more sustainable. Examples include Sweet Earth Foods' Awesome Burger and Beyond Meat's Beyond burger.

Kelly Landrieu, Whole Foods Market global coordinator, said: 'within the plant-based landscape, plant-based proteins are still a big trend with customers as more and more innovative products come to shelves.' Major companies, such as Ingredion, Beyond Meat, Bunge Loders Croklaan and HKScan are tapping into this growing market for plant-based proteins and fats in order to improve the taste of plant-based alternatives.

Flexitarian diets

According to FMI's Power of Meat 2019 report, flexitarianism can be defined as 'eating mostly a vegetarian diet, but occasionally eating meat and poultry.'

Nestlé stated that 87% of consumers in the US, including vegans and meat-eaters, are including plant-based protein into their diets, and over 50% of consumers in the UK are reportedly following a flexitarian diet. Thus, following such a diet is proving to be a major driver of the rapid growth in the plant-based market.

Consumer desire for variety, flexibility and increased ethical awareness is fuelling the need to incorporate new products – such as plant-based foods – into their diets.

Many companies in the meat industry are acknowledging the need for flexitarian blends, as Tyson Foods – usually best known for meat and poultry – predicted a huge rise in plant-based eating.

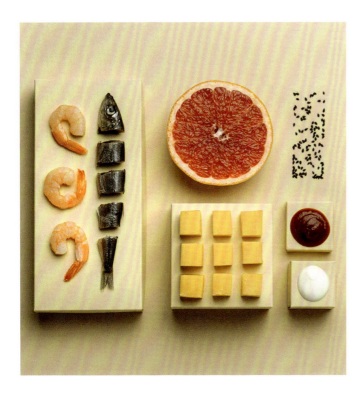

David Sprinkle, research director for Packaged Facts, said: 'A significant number of meat eaters surveyed claimed they do or would buy plant-based products, including those products that are blended with meat and plants, revealing that the meat industry faces many changes in the coming years as more consumers turn to plant-based meals and reduce their meat consumption in favour of more plants.'

Major companies jumping on the plant-based trend

According to Deloitte, existing key players in the food and beverage industry are becoming increasingly aware of small-scale disruptor brands that are developing innovation in the plant-based market. As a result, these existing companies need to consider their investment strategies for plant-based alternatives to protect their market share.

Julian Mellentin, director of food business consultancy New Nutrition Business, said: 'the plant-based food trend presents companies and brands with a major growth opportunity, but they need to choose strategy carefully.'

Key examples include Danone's £9 billion acquisition of Alpro, a major producer of plant-based alternatives, and Unilever's acquisition of The Vegetarian Butcher for an undisclosed amount.

With growth in the market evident in major food and drink companies, supermarkets are following suit. Many are presenting own-label ranges with an array of plant-based products such as Tesco's Wicked Kitchen range, Asda's plant-based range and Sainsbury's 'free-from' line of alternatives.

6 January 2020

Key Facts

- A recent study by the Federation of American Societies for Experimental Biology found the production of plant-based meat alternatives to contribute 10 times fewer greenhouse emissions than equivalent beef-based products

- Nestlé stated that 87% of consumers in the US, including vegans and meat-eaters, are including plant-based protein into their diets, and over 50% of consumers in the UK are reportedly following a flexitarian diet.

Discuss

In pairs discuss what you think are the three main factors behind the rising adoption of plant-based diets.

www.foodbev.com

Emerging trends in the plant-based industry

The plant-based revolution is here, but is it here to stay? Discover the latest growth opportunities and innovations in the plant-based sector.

The plant-based market

Over the last decade, the explosion in all things plant-based has been immense. First coined as a term in the 1980s, 'plant-based' didn't surface seriously onto the world stage until 2015. With increasing concerns about health and climate, consumer interest in both plant-based diets and plant-based lifestyles has driven a wave of product innovation in the plant-based industry around the world. Data from Mintel Global New Product Database highlights the size of that growth; between 2015 and 2021, the number of new consumer packaged goods launched with a plant-based claim has grown by nearly 700% and accounted for 12% of launches in 2021 (Mintel GNPD 2015 – 2021). It's safe to say that plant-based is now a lifestyle choice, and it's here to stay.

Looking at the last five years to May 2021, Mintel GNPD shows that the top ten companies that have launched vegan innovation globally are Danone, Aldi, dm-drogerie, Lidl, Tesco, Sainsbury's, Unilever, Marks & Spencer, Woolworths and Kellogg. These companies account for around one in ten launches of plant-based/vegan products globally – this shows how fragmented the plant-based/vegan industry still is. Interestingly, these companies have not increased their share of launches over the past five years, evidencing that smaller start-up brands continue to play a prominent role in driving growth in the vegan food market.

What does plant-based mean?

Put simply, plant-based refers to diet or consumer goods that are derived from plants (we know it sounds obvious, right?). In the main, this means fruit, vegetables, grains, pulses, nuts, oils, seeds, spices and plant-based extracts. Consumer concern over planetary environmental health and human health are the key driving factors behind the plant-based food trend. Plant-based innovations are making a splash in consumers' daily diets, such as plant-based meat substitutes/alternatives, plant-based dairy alternatives, plant-based fish/seafood alternatives and plant-based egg

substitutes. We also see plant-based claims in beauty and personal care products, household, fashion and apparel categories.

Are plant-based and vegan the same thing?

While they are similar, they have some key differences. Vegan diets eliminate all animal products, while plant-based consumption does not necessarily eliminate animal products and proteins, they instead reduce the consumption of animal-based ingredients and focus on eating more plant-based goods such as vegetables, fruit, nuts etc.

Plant-based brands have previously tapped into the vegan market but are now keen to have a more mainstream appeal focusing on flexitarians and omnivores, rather than pursuing a small segment of the vegan consumers. For example, only 3% of adults in the UK claim to follow a vegan diet.

Plant-based market scope – issues and opportunities

Plant-based meat substitutes continually press ahead towards the mainstream in many markets: half of UK and Canadian consumers engage with meat substitutes. The US trails that but still shows 39% of consumers engaging with the plant-based category.

Yet, the challenge now for Western plant-based players is generating repeat purchases, increasing consumption frequency and differentiating brands in an increasingly competitive market. The future success of the plant-based meat substitute market depends on improved taste, nutrition, environmental impact and increased value.

Is plant-based at risk of losing its healthy image?

Consumers perceive food and drink products with plant-based claims to be healthy and natural – brands that are able to deliver on those perceived benefits will have more credibility in the future. Alas, like all-natural claims before them, plant-based claims have proliferated into a wider range of sub-categories, yet such diversification could in turn threaten their credibility. In addition, reports in the media have questioned the healthiness of plant-based meat alternatives, such as the Impossible Burger compared with ground beef. This backlash could negatively impact consumers' perception of plant-based claims, leaving them to question their value.

Stand out in an increasingly crowded plant-based market by focusing on providing top consumer benefits

Focus on promoting desirable qualities, such as fruit/veg content and high protein. Protein is a key opportunity as the majority of plant-based consumers would like to see more high-protein plant-based dairy alternatives, according to Mintel's research on plant-based proteins. Food and drink companies have an opportunity to appeal to the large percentage of consumers who want to explore vegan

alternatives and add fruits, vegetables and grains into their diets – support consumers who are looking for pro-plant diets, not necessarily vegan.

Diversify plant-based protein sources

Improved variety in plant-based proteins is key for sustained market growth. Types, formats and sources of plant-based protein innovation will also continue to diversify in order to meet consumer demands for realistic alternatives to both meat and dairy. As one of the most popular plant-based products, the high use of burger substitutes has much to do with their availability and the innovations brands have made in both taste and texture. Brands can find ways to stay ahead of the competition by elevating new alternative formats to other types of meat products in the way that Impossible Foods and Beyond Meat did with burgers.

What are the latest innovations in plant-based food and drink?

Plant-based seafood innovations have recently accelerated and fish substitutes are expected to increase their plant-based market share in the near future. A variety of seafood species lend themselves to fish substitute innovation, offering more variety to consumers seeking to diversify their plant-based protein choices.

In the next decade, lab-grown dairy could take a market share between 35% and 50%, thus challenging plant-based alternatives. In the longer term, the challenges from lab-grown milk will push dairy and non-dairy to unite forces and seize the opportunity to position their hybrid products as the 'best of both worlds'.

Around a fifth of European consumers buy dairy alternatives because they can be used for baking. In the future, plant-based drinks brands will look to increase this market share as they continue to compete for new occasions beyond coffee and will use the enthusiasm over 'foamable' products to expand usage, particularly in the home cooking market.

70% of US consumers agree that food/drink companies can be leaders in protecting the environment. Moving forward, plant-based substitutes will need to work harder on their packaging sustainability to remain at a competitive advantage over animal protein products to deliver on waste reduction.

In China, 68% of adults agree that plant-based foods can help reduce the risk of the 'three highs' (high blood pressure, high cholesterol, and high blood sugar). There is a continued demand for product innovation that looks to increase the visibility of plant-based meat products and help soy-based protein products to eliminate the outdated image of soy-based foods.

August 2022

Dietary trends and plant-based perceptions in the UK

Food and drink can provide a welcome lift to our mood in challenging times. Magda Jablkowska-Citko of Toluna/Harris Interactive and Jonny Bingham of Bingham & Jones explore the results of a study conducted to understand the latest dietary trends in the UK.

From an emotional perspective, people feel very different today compared with a few years ago. This is being driven by a variety of circumstances – including the effects of the Covid-19 pandemic, the cost-of-living crisis and the war in Ukraine – and has led us to wonder, 'what are consumers doing to improve their mood or indulge?'

While some go for a walk or watch TV, two thirds of consumers say they turn to food and drink. And because there is a strong correlation between what we consume and how we feel, it is important to think about how products impact consumers in their day-to-day lives. That's why we conducted a study during the week ending 13 May 2022 to understand the latest dietary trends in the UK.

Healthy demand for healthy snacks

Our typical daily treats have changed given the situation that we find ourselves in. 58% of consumers say they find a healthy snack appealing or very appealing as a daily treat, and about four in ten consumers claim they're looking for products that are healthier, plant-based and more sustainable in nature. However, 39% admit that the current cost-of-living crisis is leading them to swap to cheaper brands – an important consideration for new product development plans.

To understand which brands are currently winning over consumers, we asked respondents to name the leading health food brands in the UK market. Overall, Graze was the leader by a wide margin – with nearly twice as many responses as the next brands, which included Naked, Weight Watchers and Quorn. The success of Graze shows that consumers desire healthy snacks and enjoy the brand's product format. For competitors, this presents an opportunity to produce cheaper alternatives with more plant-based and sustainable options.

New product development

It is challenging for brands to come up with new products, and to do so successfully requires a lot of research, development and investment. In food and drink, a great deal of innovation comes in the form of flavour, so we sought to uncover the latest flavour trends in our research. Overall, the vast majority of them are fruit-based or related to spices such as cinnamon and turmeric. Cinnamon and turmeric have been used in Indian and Chinese medicines for thousands of years, and turmeric especially is known for its healing properties.

For the most part though, it's always the same story with the consumer and flavours. Manufacturers that produce ready-

made meals for the main grocery multiples generally stay within the safety of recognised flavour profiles. Things like chicken & ham, chicken & mushroom, cheese & tomato and so on each make commercial sense because they appeal to the widest audience. Other cuisines, such as Middle Eastern or Vietnamese street food, also have a place. However, these sit within the premium segment, where there is more licence for creativity and higher prices.

In our survey data, many of the usual suspects – like mango, passion fruit, cherry and banana – continue to rank highly, as they have for years. Other, less popular flavours, such as yuzu, mangosteen and calamansi, are trending up. This puts them in the realm of 'premium,' and if used in the right way, these flavours could find some traction with consumers.

Dietary trends

In terms of specific diets, 7% of respondents say they plan to continue being or to go vegan, while 12% say the same for vegetarianism. And those numbers may continue to rise, as we noticed year-over-year growth of nine percentage points in those who are buying plant-based products. The biggest trend we noticed, however, is that 50% of consumers are either starting or continuing to reduce their meat intake. Consumers are doing this for a variety of reasons – including because it is healthier for you, better for the environment and more ethical – but for one in four, it's a midpoint en route to going vegan or vegetarian, further demonstrating that these diets are here to stay.

While the proportion who declare themselves meat eaters has declined by five percentage points since 2019, the majority of us still eat meat. What about flexitarians? We used this term on purpose and found that 28% of respondents view themselves as flexitarians, which seems like a small proportion when 50% are claiming they've reduced their meat intake. This is likely because half of meat eaters admit that they are unsure what the term 'flexitarian' means, which is an important consideration for any concept testing or communications development a brand may want to run.

Plant-based perceptions

Because consumers continue to clamour for health foods, we were keen to understand their perceptions of the health benefits of plant-based foods. As you might expect, over half of consumers felt plant-based products were healthy, but we were surprised to find that a minority felt plant-based foods were unhealthy. A variety of reasons were cited, with some saying plant-based products are highly processed, lack relevant nutrients or include additives. The remaining third of consumers were unsure – leaving room for opportunistic brands to create relevant communications that clear up any misconceptions.

We also asked respondents how likely they would be to serve plant-based products to guests. Interestingly, the consumers in our survey were quite likely to. This was most true for vegans (77%) and vegetarians (70%), but a surprising amount of meat eaters were also open to the idea (33%). Why? They believe these products are healthier and that some of the dishes can taste similar to meat-based options.

To support and guide brands and retailers in terms of how they could encourage shoppers to try plant-based foods, we asked consumers which cuisine would work best for

such a plant-based experiment in a social setting. What followed completely blew us away. We were almost certain that American and Mexican cuisines would lead the way in desirability, but it was actually British, Indian, Italian and Chinese. While most of the focus in plant-based foods has been on 'dude food,' including burgers, sausages, meatballs, mince, steaks and so on, the real opportunity lies within ready-to-eat meals with British, Chinese, Indian and Italian fare at the centre.

From a brand perspective, we know that many meat producers have decided to introduce plant-based products to their ranges – and there are many more that are considering it. But what do consumers think about this? Nearly a quarter of respondents think meat producers should not create plant-based products, largely due to fears of cross-contamination. Separating facilities between meat and plant-based is likely the best way to assuage those concerns.

Finally, we wanted to understand what plant-based products consumers are looking for that are unavailable in the marketplace. For those who are replacing meat with plant-based alternatives, they miss the taste of the real thing. And when asked to cite specific foods, they highlighted steak, cakes, cheese, fish, egg and chocolate. These results indicate that, while there are already many plant-based products in the market, there is still a lot of room for innovation.

26 July 2022

Almost a quarter of Brits are cutting back on animal products in response to 'the new normal', survey reveals

New research from The Vegan Society shows a large number of Brits have been cutting back on the amount of animal products they're consuming since the start of the Covid-19 pandemic.

Since the first national lockdown in March 2020, the society has been running consumer research to better understand how people's shopping and eating habits have changed, and what that means for the movement going forward.

Our latest research from March 2022[1] discovered that 17% of Brits have actively reduced the amount of meat they're consuming, while eight percent have cut back on dairy and/ or eggs. Three percent say they've cut back on both. For the first time this year, the survey also asked respondents about their fish intake, with six percent revealing they've cut back on the quantities of fish and seafood they're buying and consuming. In total that means almost one in four of us (23%) have minimised the amount of animal products on our plates.

When comparing this to our Changing Diets During the Covid-19 Pandemic report from the same time last year, we can see that the number of shoppers cutting back on animal products has remained steady since the pandemic started. This was also prevalent in our initial Covid-19 survey, which ran in April 2020, showing that one in five had cut down on meat consumption.

While the pandemic, Brexit and the cost-of-living crisis have all been cited as having a significant impact on our shopping habits, the top three reasons respondents gave for cutting back on animal products included health concerns (36%),

environmental reasons (28%) and animal rights issues (20%). Twelve percent said it was the cost of animal products that had motivated them to cut back, compared with eight percent in 2021, highlighting the UK's spiralling cost of living crisis.

In 2020, The Vegan Society launched the Live Vegan for Less campaign in response to growing financial concerns during the Covid-19 pandemic. This campaign has recently been relaunched to showcase that vegan living can be affordable for all as many households face rocketing energy and food bills.

Louisianna Waring, Senior Insight and Policy Officer at The Vegan Society, said: 'All three pieces of research show how the events of the last two years have highlighted to shoppers that there are more ethical and compassionate ways we can live - and these days supermarkets are only too happy to provide them.'

When it comes to what consumers are popping in their shopping baskets, it appears more and more are trying vegan alternatives for the first time with many seeing them as the 'new normal' as things return to business as usual

In a second survey[2], run in conjunction with the first, we asked 1,000 animal product reducers what vegan alternatives they have been trying. Fifty three percent said they had tried meat alternatives over lockdown, such as vegan sausages,

23%* of the UK report reducing their consumption of animal products since the start of the Covid-19 pandemic.

*final percentage derived from overlapping responses. Online survey, 1000 people in UK working age nat rep.

21-24 March 2022

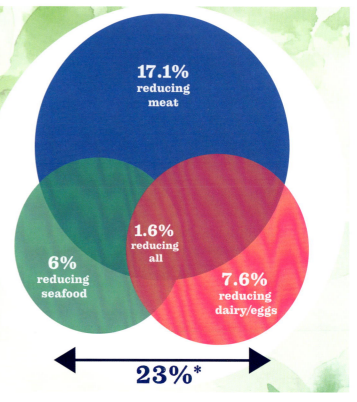

17.1% reducing meat

1.6% reducing all

6% reducing seafood

7.6% reducing dairy/eggs

23%*

Source: The Vegan Society

burgers, and bacon, with more than three-quarters (78%) stating they would continue to purchase them again in the future.

Pulses are also proving popular, with 33% of reducers trying them over lockdown, and 69% planning to buy them again. Plus, 20% of reducers told us they tried tofu for the first time during lockdown, with 61% saying they will continue buying it.

Other interesting findings include one in four (25%) trying vegan chocolate for the first time, with more than half (52%) looking to buy it again, and nine percent giving egg replacements, such as aquafaba or Crackd, a go, with 40% of those planning to purchase them again.

[1] 'Change in behaviour during the COVID-19 pandemic', conducted through Attest in March 2022, 1,000 respondents, nationally representative.

[2] 'Change in behaviour during the COVID-19 pandemic', conducted through Attest in March 2022, 1,000 respondents who said they were cutting back on animal products.

11 July 2022

Younger people feel more guilty about eating meat than older people, Vegan Society research finds

New research* by The Vegan Society has revealed that 71% of people in the UK have experienced guilt about eating meat 'some' (49%) or 'all' (22%) of the time.

And, even out of those not limiting their consumption of meat and animal products at all, 45% said they felt guilty about it 'some' or 'all' of the time.

2,000 non-vegans, including meat-eaters, those reducing their consumption of animal products, vegetarians and pescatarians, were asked questions to help understand the connection consumers make between farmed animals and their food.

The results revealed a generational gap. For those aged 18-30, 80% said they had felt guilty about eating meat. For those aged 50-65, the figure was only 59%.

Interestingly, when asked, older respondents were more likely to say they were 'very much' animal lovers (68%) compared to younger respondents (61%). The results revealed the UK is still a 'nation of animal lovers': overall 65% of the panel said they were 'very much' animal lovers, while 31% responded 'somewhat'. Just 3.3% of panellists said they had no interest in animals.

There were stark differences between respondents' level of guilt about eating different animal products. When asked to select answers for each animal product as to whether they 'ever felt guilty' for eating them:

- Out of non-vegetarian respondents (1,837 people), just 31% said they did not feel guilty for eating meat.

- Some also said they had felt guilty about consuming fish – with half of these respondents selecting 'some' (39%) or 'all' of the time (10%).

- 10% of all respondents (2,000) said they felt guilty 'all the time' about consuming dairy milk, while 29% selected 'some of the time'. 61% said they 'don't feel guilty'.

- Eating eggs had the lowest level of associated guilt, with just 8% of the total panel admitting to feeling guilty 'all the time' and 31% feeling guilty 'some of the time'.

This reflects how well cruelty is hidden in the dairy and egg industries, as many consumers do not know that they are inextricably linked to the meat industry. All animals in food systems have their lives cut cruelly short.

Editor of the society's publication *The Vegan*, Elena Orde, said: 'No one wants to contribute to suffering but unfortunately most of us were raised to think of certain animals as 'something' rather than 'someone'. Our survey demonstrates that people do recognise farmed animals as sentient. At The Vegan Society, we want to help people to reconnect with their sense of compassion and to learn how to live in alignment with their values by choosing a vegan diet and lifestyle. All animals deserve our love and respect. Our charity aims to create a welcoming and non-judgemental space for everyone to consider how their actions impact the lives of all animals, not just the ones we share our home with.'

Visit www.vegansociety.com for more information and follow The Vegan Society's socials to find support and guidance on transitioning to a vegan lifestyle.

*Survey titled 'Share your thoughts', conducted online in October 2022 via the Attest platform. 2000 non-vegan respondents, working age nationally representative for age, gender and home region.

1 November 2022

Nearly half of young people in Britain avoid eating meat with 20% following a flexitarian diet

By Molly Long

Almost 20% of young people in Britain do not eat meat, and a further 20% only do so 'occasionally' as part of a flexitarian diet, according to data gathered by YouGov.

Statistics gathered up to December 2021 showed that 5% of 18-to-24-year-olds identified as vegan or plant-based; 10% were vegetarian; and 4% were pescatarian.

The diet which has seen the sharpest uptake in recent years however is the 'flexitarian' diet. This eating regime is characterised by followers mainly eating vegetarian food, and only occasionally eating meat or fish.

Many followers of this diet do so because of its impact on the environment. Research published in Nature suggested moving to a majority plant-based flexitarian diet could reduce greenhouse gas emissions by as much as 52%.

According to YouGov data, one in five 18-to-24-year-olds follow such a diet – this is double the number reported in 2019.

The fact young people are more likely to eschew traditional meat eating habits in favour of flexitarian diets chimes with wider knowledge about Gen Z's relationship to the food industry. An EIT survey from 2021 revealed young people in this age bracket feel largely let down by the food sector.

There are many reasons why young people may feel more

conventional ways of consuming are not fit for purpose. The EIT lists reasons like food's negative impact on the climate crisis, as well as food producers and companies not doing enough to tackle other issues like health inequality, malnutrition, pollution and waste.

Flexitarianism is of growing interest to food companies too – particularly those producing plant-based meat alternatives. Marc Coloma, CEO and Co-Founder of Heura Foods, told Food Matters Live in a recent interview that his start-up 'welcomes flexitarians as regular customers'.

'We want to empower people to vote for a more sustainable food system and eat their favourite recipes without it having a toll on the environment,' he said.

Flexitarianism is on the rise more generally among British eaters too, though uptake is slower than with young people specifically. In 2019, 13% of those surveyed by YouGov reported following a flexitarian diet – this has since risen to 16%.

Beyond this diet, 2% of respondents reported following a vegan diet in 2021. This is only slightly below the estimate of how many vegans there are in the world, which Ipsos estimates is around 3% of the global population.

Some 5% of respondents reported following a vegetarian diet and 3% a pescatarian one. This means that in total, one in 10 Brits avoids eating meat completely (though some eat fish), and a quarter either doesn't eat meat or does so only occasionally.

This tracks with data released shortly after the outbreak of the Covid-19 pandemic, which suggested 25% of millennials, and 12% of Brits generally considered themselves more open to plant-based diets as a result of the coronavirus and subsequent lockdowns.

As a result of Brits' increasing acceptance of plant-based diets – and innovation in foods associated with the regime – the number of people who consider themselves mainly meat-eaters is waning, albeit slowly.

According to YouGov data, 73% of respondents were meat-eaters in 2019 and this fell to 70% in December 2021. Among young people, only 52% reported being full-time meat eaters in 2021.

20 May 2022

A third of UK consumers are willing to try lab-grown meat and a quarter would try insects

New FSA research finds that knowing these alternative proteins are safe is the top factor in encouraging consumers to try them

A survey into public perceptions of emerging alternative proteins has revealed that a third of UK consumers would try cultured meat, and a quarter would try edible insects. It also revealed a greater number – 6 in 10 of us – are willing to try plant-based products many of which are already on the market.

The Food Standards Agency research also highlights how important food safety is to consumers with it being the top factor in encouraging people to try lab-grown meat or edible insects. Assurance around food safety is already the main reason people are willing to eat plant-based proteins.

The survey comes as the FSA (Food Standards Agency) reiterates its commitment to supporting food innovation, especially where there are potential benefits for dietary health, for protecting the environment or for boosting the UK economy – but always with consumer interests and food safety as the top priority.

Alternative, or novel, sources of protein for human consumption are an emerging food and are mainly associated with plant proteins, insects and microorganisms.

Highlights of the report include:

- Awareness of alternative proteins is high amongst consumers, with 90% of respondents reporting that they had heard of plant-based proteins, 80% had heard of edible insects and 78% had heard of lab-grown meat.

- Over three quarters (77%) of respondents perceived plant-based proteins as being safe to eat compared to half (50%) for edible insects and 3 in 10 (30%) for lab-grown meat.

- Six in 10 respondents were willing to try plant-based proteins in their diet, the most common reasons were because they thought it was safe to eat (44%) and for health reasons (39%) or environmental or sustainability (36%) reasons. The biggest barrier to trying plant-based proteins was preference for traditional meats (36%).

- Around a third (34%) were willing to try lab-grown meat and just over a quarter (26%) willing to try edible insects. Environmental and sustainability were the most common reasons for trying lab-grown meat (40%) and edible insects (31%). Respondents who were unwilling to try any of the alternative proteins tested were asked whether anything could encourage them to try it:

- Two in five (42%) reported that nothing could encourage them to try lab-grown meat, but over a quarter (27%) could be persuaded if they knew it was safe to eat and 23% if they could trust that it was properly regulated.

- The majority (67%) reported that nothing could make them try edible insects. One in eight (13%) could be persuaded if they knew it was safe to eat and 11% if they looked appetising.

The FSA will be looking to bring together key industry stakeholders later this year to consider how businesses can be supported in entering this market and guide them through the FSA's existing regulatory framework and risk analysis process for the introduction of new food products.

Professor Robin May, FSA Chief Scientific Adviser, said:

'Our priority is to protect consumer interests by ensuring food is safe and what it says it is through a robust scientific process. We recognise the potential of alternative proteins for improving dietary health and as part of a sustainable food system.

'This important survey highlights that, while many consumers are considering trying alternative proteins, they will quite rightly only do so if they are confident that these products are safe and properly regulated.

'Consequently, we are working closely with businesses and trade bodies to ensure they make effective use of the FSA's existing regulatory framework so that consumers can benefit from innovative food products whilst still having full confidence in their safety.'

10 January 2022

The full report is available on the FSA (Food Standards Agency) research pages.

More companies are making lab-grown meat - so why isn't it for sale in European shops?

By Luke Hurst

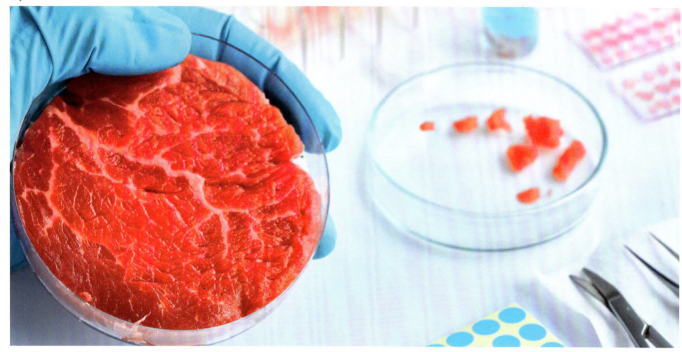

One of the big questions facing humanity right now is how to feed a global population with an increasing demand for meat, while not destroying the planet in the process.

The future of food was high on the agenda at Web Summit in Lisbon this month, and executives from two cultivated meat companies explained in detail to Euronews Next why lab-grown meat may hold the answer.

What their companies - and dozens of others - have demonstrated is that it is possible to take a tiny sample of cells from an animal, and from that sample grow meat in a lab without the need to raise, rear or kill the animal.

The process was first demonstrated to a worldwide audience nearly a decade ago, when the first lab-grown burger was eaten at a press conference in London.

And just this week, the US Food and Drug Administration (FDA) authorised the sale of lab-grown chicken for human consumption, following in the footsteps of Singapore, the first country to do so in 2020.

'You can't innovate on a cow'

If humanity is to achieve the climate goals being discussed this month at COP27, innovation and change will be needed in the animal agriculture industry.

But as Daan Luining, co-founder and CTO of lab-grown meat company Meatable, told Web Summit: 'You can't innovate on a cow'.

Instead, he is calling for more support for the growth in innovation in slaughter-free meat.

Luining, who has worked in this field for nine years with a background in cell molecular biology and tissue engineering, helped make the first lab-grown burger in 2013.

His company is developing a pork mince product, with beef mince also in the works - and they are hoping to launch their first product in Singapore next year.

Is cultivated meat the future of meat?

Advocates for lab-grown meat point to three key problems around animal agriculture, as it stands, that need fixing.

Firstly, the environmental impact is massive, accounting for around 14.5 per cent of all carbon emissions, according to the UN's Food and Agriculture Organization (FAO). There is also a strain on the resources required to produce beef.

For example, an estimated 25 kg of dry feed is needed to make a kilogram of meat from a cow, and that same kilogram requires around 15,000 litres of water, according to the Water Footprint Network.

Some studies have suggested replacing traditionally reared animal meat with lab-grown meat could cause as much as 96 per cent lower greenhouse gas emissions.

Then there's the ethical consideration. Some 80 billion animals are killed every year for human consumption, with many of those animals held in poor conditions.

Many are not slaughtered in a 'humane' manner - defined by the Humane Slaughter Association in the UK, for example, as when 'an animal is protected from avoidable excitement, pain or suffering'.

And third, there is the matter of food security. Many countries don't have the space or natural resources to rear animals to meet their population's meat demand and rely instead on imports.

Europe 'standing on the sidelines'

So why has cultured meat not taken off in Europe yet?

Luining told Euronews Next he found it 'outrageous' that the continent is 'just standing on the sidelines'.

Asked why his company was first launching its products in Singapore, he said: 'The EU is lowest on the list of priorities, because it takes so long'. 'As a start-up, we can't afford that,' he added.

The European Food Safety Authority (EFSA) regulates the industry, and there are strict criteria for a new product to be approved for sale in the bloc. Luining explained the process requires a lot of back-and-forth and he felt frustrated by a lack of clarity from the regulator.

'They're not very keen on starting the conversation and helping us understand what they actually want from us,' he said.

By contrast, he said authorities in Singapore 'have set up an entire government organ to help [us] and have been fantastic. Definitely the European Union could take note'.

The company will be gauging what the customers in Singapore think of its lab-grown meat and eventually will be able to use that experience when it comes to expanding to other markets, such as Europe.

That meat for the time being is pork mince, which can be made into a variety of products such as sausages or dumplings.

The tech - and costs - behind lab-grown meat

Because of the current state of the technology, mince meat is what most companies in this space are making right now.

That's true of Ivy Farm, a UK-based cultivated meat company that makes pork mince.

'Our technology can identify the cells that we can grow outside of the animal, basically in large fermentation tanks,' its CEO Richard Dillon told Euronews Next.

We create pure muscle, pure fat, and we can put it together to make the healthiest mincemeat -

Richard Dillon CEO, Ivy Farm

'And in the process of growing them, they replicate themselves. We then create pure muscle, pure fat, and we can put it together to make the healthiest mincemeat'.

The company came from Oxford University, where two of the original co-founders were based.

'They were looking into where there is the most research on animal mammalian culture,' Dillon said.

'And actually, it's humans. But the mammal that people eat which is closest in terms of biology to humans, is pigs. And so it was very practical,' he explained.

'Then from a commercial perspective, chicken and pork is the most eaten meat on Earth. So just the market size and the impacts that it could have globally is huge'.

But while the potential market may be there, one of the main barriers to cultivated meat hitting the supermarket shelves - aside from regulation - is cost.

'No one's ever grown mammalian cells at the large scale that would be needed to bring the costs down to feed people,' said Dillon.

The industry needs to prove it can scale, sourcing the large tanks and the materials needed to grow the cells inside them, he explained.

'That needs to essentially go through a reinvention of that supply chain to get those inputs at scale at a food-grade cost instead of a biopharmaceutical cost.'

He said there have been great strides made since the first lab-grown burger was demonstrated. That burger cost around €250,000 to produce.

'We could do the equivalent now for less than $100 (€100). And we're still at a very small pilot scale. So it's going to be orders of magnitude with the costs coming down over the next two years'.

Last updated: 18 November 2022

www.euronews.com

Useful Websites

www.bioecoactual.com

www.eufic.com

www.euronews.com

www.foodbev.com

www.foodgov.uk

www.foodmatterslive.com

www.forgerecycling.co.uk

www.independent.co.uk

www.mintel.com

www.theconversation.com

www.theguardian.com

www.thehumaneleague.org.uk

www.vegansociety.com

www.webber-nutrition.co.uk

www.wildmag.co.uk

www.yougov.co.uk

Further Reading

References

Page 22-23

1. Webster, J., Greenwood, D. C., & Cade, J. E. (2022). Risk of hip fracture in meat-eaters, pescatarians, and vegetarians: results from the UK Women's Cohort Study. BMC medicine, 20(1), 1-10.

2. Kanis, J. A., Cooper, C., Rizzoli, R., & Reginster, J. Y. (2019). European guidance for the diagnosis and management of osteoporosis in postmenopausal women. Osteoporosis International, 30(1), 3-44.

3. World Health Organization. (2021). Plant-based diets and their impact on health, sustainability and the environment: a review of the evidence: WHO European Office for the Prevention and Control of Noncommunicable Diseases. Copenhagen: WHO Regional Office for Europe.

Page 36-37

[1]'Change in behaviour during the COVID-19 pandemic', conducted through Attest in March 2022, 1,000 respondents, nationally representative.

[2]'Change in behaviour during the COVID-19 pandemic', conducted through Attest in March 2022, 1,000 respondents who said they were cutting back on animal products.

Page 39

https://www.food.gov.uk/research/behaviour-and-perception/survey-of-consumer-perceptions-of-alternative-or-novel-sources-of-protein

Amino acids

Amino acids are molecules that combine to form proteins. They are essential to the body for many functions including tissue repair and nutrient absorption.

Diet

The variety of foods and drink that someone consumes on a regular basis. The phrase 'on a diet' is also often used to refer to a period of controlling what one eats while trying to lose weight.

Fibre

Dietary fibre (sometimes called 'roughage') is the part of fruit, vegetables and wholefoods which cannot be digested by the body. It aids digestion by giving the gut bulk to squeeze against in order to move food through the digestive system. There are two types of fibre: soluble and insoluble.

Flexitarian

Sometimes known as 'semi' or 'demi' vegetarian. A term coined to describe a diet which is mostly vegetarian but occasionally includes meat consumption, although this is often limited to only fish or white meat.

Fruitarian

A diet related to veganism that consists primarily of raw fruits. Some fruitarians are more flexible than others and also eat some vegetables, nuts and seeds.

Lab-grown meat

Also known as 'cultivated' or 'cultured' meat, lab-grown meat is real meat grown directly from muscle cells harvested from living animals.

Meat substitute

Also referred to as meat analogues, meat substitutes imitate the texture and quality of meat but are made from non-animal products such as soya, tofu, mycoprotein or similar. Meat substitutes are popular with some vegetarians as sources of fibre and protein: others, however, dislike the taste and texture of anything resembling meat.

Nutrition

The provision of materials needed by the body for growth, maintenance and sustaining life. Commonly when people talk about nutrition, they are referring to the healthy and balanced diet we all need to eat in order for the body to function properly.

Omnivore

An omnivore's diet includes both plants and animals.

Pescatarian

A term sometimes used to describe someone who excludes all meat from their diet with the exception of fish. Some people who eat fish and no other meat choose to refer to

Glossary

themselves as vegetarians, however, because the term 'pescatarian' is not widely used or understood. However, eating fish means they do not follow a 100% vegetarian diet.

Plant based diet

A plant-based diet is any diet that is based either wholly or predominantly on foods derived from plants.

Protein

Proteins are chains of amino acids that allow the body to build and repair body tissue. Protein is found in dairy foods, meat, fish and soya beans.

Quorn

Quorn is the well-known brand name of a large vegetarian food range. Quorn products are made from a type of fungus called mycoprotein.

Soya

A bushy herb native to Asia. The seed from the soybean plant is an excellent source of protein and is often used as a meat substitute.

Tofu

Tofu, sometimes called bean curd or soybean curd, is a creamy, high-protein, low-fat soy product typically sold in blocks

Vegan

Vegans oppose the use of animal food products as well as material or by-products which are produced by an animal; they exclude meat, fish, poultry, dairy products, eggs and honey from their diet.

Vegetarian

Someone who does not eat meat, fish, poultry or any slaughterhouse by-product such as gelatine. There are different types of vegetarian, including lacto-ovo vegetarians, who eat both eggs and dairy; ovo vegetarians, who eat eggs but not dairy; and lacto vegetarians, who eat dairy but not eggs.

Vitamins

Organic compounds that are essential to the body, but only in very small quantities. Most of the vitamins and minerals we need are provided through a balanced diet: however, some people choose to take additional vitamin supplements.

Index